Preface

In view of the growing importance of services in the economy, the European Commission has found it important to draw the attention of policy makers on the necessity to improve the framework conditions for the operation of services adding value to the economy.

Among these activities, Business Services are recognised to hold the major potential for furthering growth in both employment and GNP through their input to all economic activities. A strong and competitive European Business Services sector will improve the competitiveness of both manufacturing industry and service activities.

The efforts of the European Commission to focus and initiate the debate on these dynamic relations have resulted in the enclosed documentation.

Our first attempt to analyse the situation of Business Services is contained in the Commission Report from April 1998. It was followed up by a Commission Communication from September 1998 creating an EU policy in the area. These policy initiatives where endorsed by the Industry Council in November 1998 establishing a platform for the implementation of concrete actions and providing guidance for our future initiatives in this field.

To this end, we have chosen to introduce the subject by the shortest and most operational document, namely the Council Conclusions. The Commission Communication and the Report should thus be considered interpretative contributions to the implementation of the Council Conclusions.

The texts have been available on the Internet since their approval. However, we feel that a paper version of the texts is also necessary in order to reach the broadest possible range of interested parties.

It is my sincere hope that this collection of documents will provide the reader with some useful background and basic statistical information in order to participate in the European debate on the future of Business Services.

Concurrently with this documentation, DGIII is launching a more detailed academic analysis contained in the DGIII publication under the title: 'Business Services in European Industry: Growth, Employment and Competitiveness'. This publication is also available from the Office for Official Publications of the European Communities.

Magnus Lemmel

Acting Director General, European Commission, DGIII Industry

The Contribution of Business Services to Industrial Performance

A Common Policy Framework

EUROPEAN COMMISSION
DG III – Industry

A great deal of additional information on the European Union is available on the Internet.
It can be accessed through the Europa server (http://europa.eu.int).

Cataloguing data can be found at the end of this publication.

Luxembourg: Office for Official Publications of the European Communities, 1999

ISBN 92-828-6670-X

Printed in Italy

Table of contents

1

Council Conclusions
on Business Services
and their Contribution to the Competitiveness
of European Industry

THE COUNCIL

Noting with interest:

- the Commission Communication on "The Contribution of Business Services to Industrial Performance - A Common Policy Framework" [1] and the Commission Staff working paper "Report to the Council on Industrial Competitiveness and Business Services" [2];

Recalling:

- the White Paper of the Commission on Growth, Competitiveness and Employment [3];

- the Council Conclusions of 22 April 1994 on the White paper: Improving the Competitiveness of European Industry [4];

- the Council Conclusions of 7 April 1995 on the Industrial Competitiveness Policy for the European Union [5];

- the Council Conclusions of 6-7 November 1995 concerning Industrial Competitiveness and Business Services [6];

- the Council Conclusions of 14 November 1996 on Benchmarking the Competitiveness of European Industry [7];

Recognising that:

- a thriving Business Services sector is of major importance for the competitiveness of European Industry and an important factor in the creation of employment and lasting economic growth;

- the Business Services sector has been identified as one of the economic sectors with the highest potential for growth in both added value and employment;

- competitive Business Services can help SMEs to innovate and grow;

Considering:

- that the proposed policy framework for Business Services, described in the above mentioned Commission Communication can open up new opportunities for improving the competitiveness of European Industry;

[1]   Doc. 11419/98 - COM (98) 534 final.

[2]   Doc. 8211/98 ECO 52 - SEC(98) 735.

[3]   OJ C 91, 28.3.1994, p. 124 - COM(93) 700.

[4]   Doc. 6519/94 PV/CONS 24 IND 2

[5]   Doc. 6469/95 PV/CONS 21 IND 2

[6]   Doc. 11282/95 PV/CONS 60 IND 4.

[7]   Doc. 11409/96 PV/CONS 66 IND 11.

- that barriers have to be identified and removed in order to improve the competitiveness of Business Services in accordance with the Community Policy on industrial competitiveness;

Supporting the following objectives:

- improving knowledge of the situation of Business Services in the European Union and their contribution to industrial performance;
- taking further steps towards deepening the Internal Market and enhancing fair competition between enterprises in the Business Services sector;
- improving the application of existing EU policies to Business Services in order to strengthen their competitiveness and that of their clients;

I. INVITES THE COMMISSION AND THE MEMBER STATES WITHIN THEIR RESPECTIVE COMPETENCES TO:

a) improve the statistical regulatory framework at both Community and national level in order to remedy the major shortcomings in existing statistics on Business Services, in particular with regard to Council Regulation 58/97 on Structural Business statistics, and to consider - where appropriate and within existing budgetary frameworks - how to ensure a better balance between data collection in manufacturing and service sectors;

b) collect data and analyse the links between qualifications, skills, labour conditions and human capital productivity in order to understand how employment in the Business Services sector is created, how this affects job creation in other sectors of the economy, and to identify future needs;

c) ensure the systematic data collection, monitoring and the carrying out of analyses on services adding value to Industry by establishing a network of all existing parties without adding administrative burdens;

d) undertake a review of any barriers to entry to the Single Market with a view to their removal;

e) recognize and raise awareness of the potential contribution of:

- the 5th Framework Programme on research and development,
- the Multi-annual Programme for SMEs,
- the First Action Plan on Innovation,
- the Structural Funds,
- the European public procurement regulatory framework,
- the 1998 National Action Plans for employment
- other relevant Community policies

to the improvement of the Business Services sector and its contribution to the competitiveness of European Industry;

f) promote the creation of cooperation networks between Business Services suppliers;

g) endeavour to secure the opening of third country markets in the context of the GATS 2000 round of negotiations;

II. CALLS UPON THE COMMISSION TO:

a) provide an inventory of all legislation relating specifically and exclusively to the Business Services sector;

b) analyse continuously and benchmark existing practices in the following areas:

- European and national promotion of Business Services,
- development of Business Services in specific regions, particularly in least favoured regions,
- interaction between public administrations and Business Services;

c) analyse how Business Services are affected, how they will be transformed and which kind of Business Services are likely to be created by Information Society technologies and their applications;

d) investigate the possibilities of extending activities concerning Business Services to other services adding value to Industry;

e) analyse continuously the structure of the European Business Services market in order to avoid distortion of competition;

f) submit regular progress reports to the Council;

III. UNDERTAKES TO:

- continue examination of the Commission Communication on Business Services with a view to analysing further the opportunities for appropriate policy measures and report to an Industry Council in 1999;

- discuss regularly, in connection with the competitiveness debate, progress in the above mentioned fields and to consider new policy initiatives.

COMMUNICATION FROM THE COMMISSION

The Contribution of Business Services to Industrial Performance
A Common Policy Framework

2

Preface

The Industry Council in its Conclusions of the 6-7/11/1995 invited the Commission to analyse the situation of Business Services from the point of view of their contribution to industrial competitiveness and job creation. It further asked the Commission to produce a Communication on the future of Business Services and to consider appropriate policy actions.

A detailed factual description and analysis of the situation of Business Services is contained in the Commission Staff Working Paper "Industrial Competitiveness and Business Services" submitted to the Council in April 1998. The present Communication is the operational follow-up to this document which should be considered an integral part of the Communication.

The key political messages of this Communication are the following :

There is an urgent need to improve data and information on Business Services and their contribution to European competitiveness and job creation.

Market access barriers for Business Services in the Member States must be identified and be removed.

Optimal conditions must be created to ensure that the Business Services sector contributes to employment creation both in the sector itself and indirectly by its added value input into Industry. Compared to the United States there could be an untapped potential of more than 3 million jobs in the Business Services sector.

The real challenges are :

▶ To match skills to knowledge-based Business Services.

▶ To explore the huge potential of European export by putting Business Services companies at the forefront in international competition.

▶ To ensure that our Business Services companies are clustering and operating in networks so the full potential of access to innovation and the capital market is realised.

▶ To contribute to competitiveness, growth and innovation of Industry and in particular of SMEs by promoting their use of Business Services.

Table of contents

Chapter 1 | Introduction

In its Conclusions of the 6-7/11/1995, the Industry Council invited the Commission to carry out an analysis of the situation of Business Services from the point of view of their contribution to the competitiveness of European enterprises and job creation. The result of this analysis was presented to the Council in a Report from the Commission Services on Industrial Competitiveness and Business Services [1].

The Council Conclusions furthermore invited the Commission to examine how national and Community policies can contribute to improving the framework conditions within which Business Services operate and to assess the contribution of Business Services to the internationalisation of business, in particular of SMEs. Finally, the Commission was invited to produce a Communication on the future of Business Services in the European Union, focusing particularly on the arguments for and against a policy on the subject.

The present Communication represents the follow-up to these requests. Following the Report on Industrial Competitiveness and Business Services, it expands the economic justifications for a policy on Business Services and further examines the policy issue that the Report broadly identified as needing treatment.

As stated in the Report, the key importance of Business Services lies in their dynamic links and their contribution to the competitiveness of EU Industry [2]. An important element in EU competitiveness policy is to promote intangible investment (knowledge-creation, quality, innovation, management etc). Business Services are often required to supply key elements of such investments. Hence, to promote intangible investments also requires the promotion of those services.

Business Services are of major importance in helping the SME sector realise its potential contribution to innovation and growth. There is evidence that some of the most dynamic SME already make use of Business Services to perform the functions that can not be undertaken in-house. In the face of the pressures of internationalisation, greater use of these services by a wider range of SMEs needs to be encouraged.

The providers of Business Services are, themselves, often small enterprises, which require the right environment to be able to flourish. This consideration has to be borne in mind as a critical element in any moves to encourage the further development of the sector.

With the growing integration of Business Services into manufacturing (and vice versa) and their importance for overall economic development, policy on industrial competitiveness needs to be extended and targeted on Business Services. It is because of these interactions (which will be further developed in Chapter 4) that the Commission in this Communication builds on the overall policy framework guiding EU competitiveness policy, including its impact on employment and economic growth [3].

The policy actions treated in this Communication are in general covering all Business Services. However, when dealing with the abolition of national market access restrictions which are specific to individual activities and vary from country to country, this horizontal approach is not feasible.

Compared with former scattered and non-coordinated initiatives in this field, not only the supply of Business Services is treated but also the demand side in order to ensure that the interests of client industries are taken into account in a coherent supply/demand side approach, permitting the anticipation of future needs for services and the emergence of new types of Business Services.

[1] Doc. Sec (1998)735 of 29/4/1998.

[2] In the following, "Industry" is defined as manufacturing and services activities supplied on a market basis whether integrated into each other or not.

[3] See Annex 1. for references.

It should be noted that since this Communication constitutes a first attempt in putting together a policy framework in an area characterised by a lack of sufficiently disaggregated and credible economic information, priority at this stage is given to the systematic collection of statistical data, analysis and research. A refinement, a deepening and an extension of policy actions should take place concurrently with the increased availability of data and analytical material, appropriate to the implementation of policy decisions.

The Commission will periodically report back to the Council on progress in this field, together with the implications for policy making. Furthermore, depending on the result of feasibility studies already undertaken, the extension of policy actions to other services to Industry such as industrial training, logistics and contract research will be considered in a next phase.

The policy objectives of this Communication are synthesised in the box below.

It is underlined that the Commission is *not proposing a new specific policy on Business Services*. What is sought is the implementation in a coherent framework of existing policies which already affect Business Services.

Policy objectives

To strengthen the competitiveness of European Industry by improving the framework in which Business Services function to the benefit of the entire Industry Value Added Chain by :

① **Facilitating decision making:** To create a comprehensive theoretical and analytical basis on which to undertake a continuous monitoring of the situation of Business Services in order to ensure a sufficient background for decision makers at the enterprise, public administration and political level.

② **Applying Community policies:** To improve the business environment in which Business Services and their clients work by using existing Community policy instruments to enhance competitiveness. The most important of these policies are Enterprise Policy and the creation of a favourable environment for SMEs, the Information Society and Electronic Commerce, RDT, Training, Internal Market and Public Procurement, GATS, Structural Policy, Competition policy and Quality Assurance.

| Chapter 2 | **Definition and classification of Business Services** | 2 |

Business Services consist of many different activities. They include highly advanced consultancy services like management consultancy or computer services, professional services like engineering and legal services, marketing services like advertising or fairs and exhibitions, labour intensive services like personnel services, and operational services like cleaning and security services. This heterogeneous panorama of Business Services is explained by the different functional characteristics of enterprises which purchase these services: management, administration, production, ICT, marketing, personnel, security, cleaning etc. For any key enterprise function, a corresponding Business Service exists. They are characterised by an interactive co-production process between the supply and demand side with the overall purpose of improving the competitiveness of the client. A detailed definition of Business Services, listing all the activities is given in the Report on Industrial Competitiveness and Business Services. For practical and illustrative reasons, the main Business Services activities and their classification are shown below:

▶ **Definition of Business Services according to NACE Rev. 1. classification***

Classification Of NACE activities	Services	Most important activities
72.1-6	Computer	▶ Hardware consultancy ▶ Software consultancy ▶ Data processing ▶ Data base activities
74.11, 74.12,74.14	Professional	▶ Legal activities ▶ Accounting and tax consultancy ▶ Management consulting
74.13, 74.4	Marketing	▶ Market research ▶ Advertising
74.2, 74.3	Technical	▶ Architectural activities ▶ Engineering activities ▶ Technical testing and analysis
71.1, 71.21–23, 71.31-33	Leasing and renting	▶ Renting of transport and construction equipment ▶ Renting of office machinery incl. computers
74.5	Labour recruitment	▶ Labour recruitment and provision of personnel
74.6, 74.7	Operational	▶ Security activities ▶ Industrial cleaning
74.81–84	Other	▶ Secretarial and translation activities ▶ Packaging activities ▶ Fairs and Exhibitions

* This definition is in accordance with the EUROSTAT publication 'Business Services in Europe' from 1995. It should be noted that NACE classes 70 (real estate services), 73 (research and development) and subclass 74.15 (holding companies) are not included in this definition.

Chapter 3

Key performance figures for Business Services

The Report on Industrial Competitiveness and Business Services underlined the serious gap in basic statistical data on Business Services. Based on a number of different sources, extrapolations and estimates have been made giving some key figures which should be treated with a certain caution until further work has been done in this field (see chapter 5). The main problem is that comparisons between EU Member States are hampered by an uneven geographical statistical coverage and different levels of aggregation of services sectors.

This chapter only concerns those Business Services purchased outside a company to the exclusion of the those supplied in-house.

A. Size and growth of Business Services

Table 1 in annex 2 shows the basic statistics for Business Services in Europe. The sector employs more than 11.5 million people and contributes to more than 850 billion ECU value added. This represents 8.5% of total employment and 15.3 % of value added. The sector is organised in many small firms (more than 2.5 million) operating mainly in national markets.

Annual growth rates shown in table 2 in annex 2 demonstrates the very impressive growth of Business Services during the last years. Both employment and value added indicators amount to an annual growth of around 5.5% in Business Services, while the total economy grew at 0.4% in employment and 1.5% in value added. This rapid growth can partly be explained by an increased recourse to outsourcing of Business Services' activities but it is believed that the main reason lies in Industry's demand for new, advanced, knowledge-based and specialised services, cfr chapter 4.

B. Comparisons to other sectors of the economy

1. Value added

The following comparisons are useful in order to understand the attention which should be given to the Business Services sector:

- Business Services generate more value added (15.3%) than banking, insurance, transport and communication services altogether (12.1%).

- Value added from the Business Services to the economy is around 72% of that from the manufacturing industry and six times as much as agriculture.

Figure 1 in annex 3 compares gross value added of Business Services to other major economic sectors.

2. Employment

In terms of employment, the absolute figure is equal to the employment in banking, insurance, transport and communication services altogether. It is close to the total employment in wholesale and retail trade. As opposed to these services, many Business Services are of high value added with well-paying jobs.

Figure 2 in annex 3 compares employment in Business Services to other major economic sectors.

The difference between the percentages in value added and employment illustrates the *high relative* productivity level in Business Services compared to the situation in other services and a productivity level at least similar to the one in manufacturing.

Relative employment figures and relative productivity levels are, however, not the only relevant factors in assessing the importance of Business Services for the creation of employment.

Estimates of the potential growth in this sector could be based on the fact that over 14 years (1980-1994), employment has grown by 5.5 % per year at an average, higher than in any other sector of the economy and there are no reasons to believe that this pattern will change. On the contrary, technological development and internationalisation will create new Business Services activities with further prospects for job-creation.

3. Room for growth

From the above it can be concluded that Business Services are one of the few sectors of the economy where high productivity levels go hand in hand with strong employment growth and that this trend is expected to continue.

These facts give no reasons for complacency. There is an unused potential for Business Services to contribute to competitiveness, growth and employment. As mentioned, their value added input is only around 72% of the input from manufacturing. This picture should be compared to the situation in the USA where Business Services accounts for 106% of manufacturing industry value added. (See table 3 in annex 2, other comparisons between some representative European countries and the USA are given in annex 4). *This room for manoeuvre can only be filled by giving more political attention to an improvement of the framework conditions in which Business Services are functioning at EU Level.*

Chapter 4 | Why Business Services are important to industrial competitiveness and economic growth

A. Basic relationships

The reasons for Industry's recourse to Business Services are based on a heterogeneous set of factors inherent in the performance of Business Services such as improved flexibility, greater specialisation, product differentiation tailored to customers needs, concentration on core activities, change in internal organisation, cost reductions, improved quality, better access to knowledge, skills, expertise and new technology, search for new markets (internationalisation) etc.

It is the performance of this set of factors that lead to increases in productivity, competition and employment, the 3 basic elements of industrial competitiveness and economic growth.

These factors are directly related to 4 main reasons which have been identified as explanation for the economic importance of Business Services and which are investigated below under points B-E.

> **Scene of investigation**
>
> ▶ Dynamic relations to Industry
>
> ▶ Creation of competitive advantages
>
> ▶ Development of knowledge and innovation
>
> ▶ Possibilities for job-creation

The relationships mentioned above can be illustrated in annex 5.

B. Dynamic relations to Industry

One of the reasons for the rapid growth of Business Services over the last two decades is that functions that were previously performed inside manufacturing industries are now outsourced, based on the set of factors mentioned above. This is however, not the main reason for growth of value added and employment in the sector. It is not simply a replacement of in-house services by out-house services.

As mentioned in the introduction, *their key importance* lies in their dynamic links and contributions to the competitiveness of European enterprises, because of their growing integration into industrial production.

Business Services are required in order to cope with industrial change. Business Services are needed by enterprises to adapt their production chain in a more flexible way, to improve the quality of the human and technological production factors, to create product differentiation, to cope with rapid technological development and to face the more complex and international markets. These intangible elements and inputs to the value added chain are becoming more important than the traditional tangible investments.

An important dynamic relationship and mutual reinforcement exists between Business Services and Industry. The growth of Business Services is due to an increased demand from the Industry and growth in Industry is increasingly linked to their own use of Business Services. This relationship drives growth and employment, and therefore needs more attention from policy decision-makers.

It is becoming increasingly well understood that *a great number of cost pressures on Industry are generated not only within manufacturing but in the Business Services sector.* These 'input services' are in many cases less competitive in Europe than in the USA and other advanced economies and the causes for this need to be addressed (see chapter 5 on policy actions).

The effect on downstream activities reduce the competitiveness of European enterprises as a whole which is the central argument for improving the framework conditions in which Business Services and their clients operate.

C. Creation of competitive advantages

Three competitive advantages due to the use of Business Services can be identified: lower prices, higher quality and more internationalisation.

1. Lower prices

The existence of well-developed markets for Business Services reduce cost pressures on Industry due to productivity improvements, conversion of fixed costs into variable costs and creation of new demands for Business Services which lead to more competition and lower prices.

2. Higher quality

The way in which Business Services contribute to industrial quality is not only related to specialisation but also to the fact that some services directly allow the manufacturing and service industries to improve their own quality standards in processes and products. Some Business Services like *quality control, certification, design or engineering services* contribute to good quality results and product differentiation. Others like advertising, market research or fairs and exhibitions allow *key information inputs* to be received from clients and competitors that feed into responses to product weakness, quality issues, enhanced differentiation and entrepreneurial strategies that address market needs. The fact that many of these services are now outsourced brings into play competitive processes which increase the quality and choice available, especially where the dynamic and innovative potential of smaller Business Services providers is given sufficient scope.

3. Internationalisation

Three factors contribute to easier access for client companies to foreign markets.

- Business Services reinforce enterprise competitiveness, preparing the Business Services clients for more competition abroad. In addition, some specific Business Services are required *to define, plan and develop an international strategy.* (Management consultancy, fairs and exhibition, market research and advertising IT services etc.) This type of assistance can be particularly significant for smaller enterprises venturing into new markets.

- Business Services facilitate dealing with barriers to trade. Many Business Services help to overcome differences in legal, economic and cultural barriers both within and outside of the Single Market. Whereas the regulatory barriers within the Single Market must be addressed, the other barriers can only be overcome with the help of such services as those of management consultancy, translation and interpreting, IT-specialists, lawyers, etc.

- Direct foreign investment and inter and intra-firm trade in Business Services permit clients to have access to multinational Business Services firms. Even direct trade, which is a secondary way of Business Services internationalisation, is increasing at a high growth rate, much higher than most of other services and manufacturing.

D. Development of knowledge and innovation

Most Business Services are knowledge intensive services. They provide strategic information permitting Industry to adapt to technological development, internationalisation and an increasingly complex society.

Thus, they are a key factor for technological innovation. In order for a client company to avail itself of Business Services, new technology often has to be introduced, leading to an update of the technological industrial base. At the same time, Business Services increase the effectiveness of technological inputs since advanced services like IT-services allow a better use of existing technology.

On the other hand, new technologies allow expansion of Business Services markets by increasing their tradability, in particular those which have been constrained by geographical or time proximity of production and consumption. New technology leads to better performing Business Services and vice-versa.

For these reasons, RDT, IT, and innovation policies need to focus on the building of a strong technological base for innovation in Business Services. Since Europe clearly is behind the United States in development of new technologies and in advanced Business Services, a potential margin exists for the promotion of policy actions to stimulate the innovation capacity of the market.

Business Services also contribute greatly to product and process innovation of a non-technical kind. This arises both directly because of the nature of the services provided to other enterprises and indirectly through the effects of competition generated by enterprises that have benefited from the services provided. In this way effective Business Services stimulate a whole range of innovative activities.

E. Possibilities for job-creation

A dynamic and thriving Business Services sector is important as a creator of employment in its own right (see previous chapter). However, *its main importance lies in its indirect job-creation potential by its added value input into Industry, which generates more economic activity* which in turn creates new employment opportunities.

Furthermore, the accumulation of skills and specialised expertise in Business Services, particularly in labour recruitment services, allows a better selection, contracting, training, recycling, and management of personnel. It should, however, be kept in mind that the expansion in labour recruitment services, in so far as it represents personnel working ad interim in other sectors of the economy, does not indicate a growth of this sector per se, but rather a change in contractual arrangements.

Rough estimates show that about 20% more persons are employed in in-house Business Services' activities than in independent Business Services companies. It indicates that there is room for further outsourcing of Business Services activities with the positive effects on productivity *and the impact on indirect job-creation*. In order to fully understand this process and the policy implications, it is necessary to undertake research on Industry's demand for Business Services. To obtain the complete picture, better data on the supply (independent Business Services) and the demand (for both out-house and in-house Business Services) must be provided.

The overall purpose of creating a policy framework for Business Services is to reinforce the dynamic links between Business Services and economic performance in general. The previous chapters treated the economic justification for the creation of a policy on Business Services. This chapter justifies and defines the content of the policy that the Commission proposes for improving the situation of Business Services based on the policy on industrial competitiveness.

When this policy is applied to Business Services the following six major objectives are emerging:

A▸ Improving productivity;

B▸ Promotion of employment possibilities;

C▸ Improving competition in the Business Services sector;

D▸ Promotion of industrial cooperation between Business Services suppliers;

E▸ Promotion of Business Services;

F▸ Encouraging modernisation of public administrations.

A number of EU policies contribute to industrial competitiveness. Below it will be shown how, to various extents, these policies can be applied to the six above-mentioned objectives.

In the development of a Business Services policy, the challenge is to implement policies in a coherent framework related to each of the six major objectives. When these policies are implemented under a global vision, synergies and mutual reinforcement of actions are created. This demands a coordination effort in all the stages of policy planning and application, follow-up and evaluation. One or several independent policies can not resolve what a coordinated action in the implementation of a multitude of policies in a coherent framework can.

Objective A | **Improving productivity**

Because of the intangible nature of Business Services, measurement of productivity raises difficult problems. It is necessary to distinguish between productivity gains by suppliers of Business Services in the production and distribution of their own services (cf. chapter 3) and productivity gains in the economy as a whole, resulting from the applications of Business Services. Thus, even if Business Services themselves are not gaining in productivity, they may be causing productivity gains elsewhere of great overall benefit to the economy. To gain better knowledge of this process, new indicators and methodologies on how to measure must be created.

Furthermore, it is necessary to gain better knowledge on certain barriers to productivity improvements (labour market rigidities, small and fragmented markets, heavy administrative burdens etc) and to explore the ways in which training, knowledge, information technology and innovation contributes to the key relationship between Business Services and industrial productivity.

The expansion of the Business Services sector has to a large extent been brought about by continuous changes in product development much of which is driven by the improvement in intellectual capital. Education, training and other human resources development policies will need to remain in focus permanently as will the need for their rapid modification in the light of competitive changes in product and other market development.

The following four actions would support the objective of improving industrial productivity. These are related to several existing EU policies: Data and information collection, quality promotion, RDT and innovation and IT-policy.

Action 1

To create new instruments for measuring productivity

Measures:

▶ To find new indicators for price/quality ratio, real inflation, output growth, etc, creating a new statistical methodology for measuring input and output in each Business Services activity.

▶ To find indicators and to measure Business Services role in improving the productivity of their clients and, therefore, of the whole economic system.

▶ To analyse other factors that determine the demand for Business Services, including the existence of market failures in the relevant markets and the policy responses to them.

Action 2

To identify and evaluate barriers to productivity improvements

Measures:

▶ To assess the role of Business Services in overcoming existing barriers to improved productivity in the economy.

▶ To analyse the effects of outsourcing on the productivity of Industry.

Action 3

To improve the quality of human resources

Measures:

▶ To analyse qualifications, skills and labour conditions in Business Services companies and identify future needs.

▶ To analyse how those Business Services activities related to human resources (management consultancy, labour recruitment, etc) contribute to improving the human capital productivity in Industry.

▶ To promote the elaboration of a European system of quality control of training, based on an approach similar to that of process and product quality standards and backed up by certification taking into account the need to focus on skills transferability, making them more transparent for both workers and employers.

Action 4

To foster innovation

Measures:

▶ To create awareness and facilitate Business services companies' participation in projects that promote innovation in service provision, including those under the 5th Framework Programme and the Multi-annual Programme for SMEs.

▶ To facilitate Business services companies participation in actions under the First Action Plan on Innovation, in particular in actions promoting Business Services application of IT-technologies through demonstration and pilot projects, workshops, etc.

Objective B Promotion of employment possibilities

Most of the actions and measures mentioned above under the objective on improving productivity are necessary but not sufficient for the creation of all the jobs that Business Services can provide. Thus, actions and measures under this Objective should be seen as complementary.

As illustrated in chapters 3 and 4, the Business Services sector is probably the economic sector with the highest potential for job creation, not only in its own right but particularly by their added value input to Industry with its positive effects on employment, competitiveness and growth in Industry. It has also been illustrated that there is room for further job-creation. However, to get better understanding of these interactions and mechanisms, reliable statistical and analytical data are necessary.

Furthermore, advantages should be taken of other job creation schemes with a direct impact on Business Services, such as the new possibilities opened up by the recently adopted Employment Guidelines and the new orientations in the European Social Fund.

The following three actions would support this objective. The actions are related to existing EU policies on: Data and information collection, employment policy coordination, Information Society and training under the Social Fund.

Action 1

To improve knowledge about the job creation potential of Business services

Measure:

▶ To collect data and analyse relationships between qualifications, skills and labour conditions in order to understand how employment in the Business Services sector is created and how this affect job creation in other sectors of the economy.

Action 2

Co-ordination of national employment policies

Measure:

▶ To create awareness in Business Services organisations and companies of the new possibilities which will follow from the guidelines of the 1998 National Action Plans for employment.

▶ To remove barriers to mobility and promote access to education and training through development at distance learning, University/School/Industry partnership and the exchange of best practices.

Action 3

To encourage employment development in Business Services through the European Social Fund and other human resources related programmes

Measures:

▶ To create a co-ordinated and systematic employment and training scheme, for example in the form of an ICT based job-watching scheme, in order to link education, training and employment at European level.

▶ To improve the awareness of Business Services organisations and companies of the possibilities for support from the European Social Fund under its new priorities.

▶ To develop Business Services training and education infrastructure, particularly in the context of local development and the promotion of employment and training in the third system of employment (cooperatives, mutualities, etc).

Objective C Improving competition in the Business Services sector

As illustrated in chapter 4, Business Services provide significant intangible inputs needed by European enterprises to compete in global and complex markets. Thus, one major objective of this Communication is to assist European enterprises in identifying and using, in an efficient way, the Business Services they need. One of the more serious obstacles to improved competition between providers of Business Services is the lack of transparency of the quality of the service provided. For fear of the unknown, clients of Business Services often tend to deal with service providers they already know, thus making it difficult for newcomers to access the market. This issue raises questions about the role of regulations in ensuring standards and fairplay, which always has to be balanced with an appreciation of the need to avoid imposing regulatory burdens on enterprises.

Furthermore, the very nature of the Internal Market implies that any Business Service lawfully provided in the country of establishment should in principle be freely available to clients in other Member States, without the need to verify in each instance whether it is compatible with regulatory, administrative, professional provisions or other barriers in the client country. The likely reduction that this would bring about in the costs of complying will assist Business Services providers in extending their activities beyond their national borders, thereby increasing competition within the Internal Market and internationally, stimulating yet more efficient provision of Business Services to the benefit of their clients. To this end, it is necessary to analyse all barriers to entry, such as price regulation, tariffs, technical standards, licences, product differentiation, excess capacity, etc. This identification of lack of application of Internal Market principles will together with the application of the competition rules of the Treaty and/or national competition rules help to eliminate most of the barriers.

Competition in the market would also be improved by new more efficient and flexible public procurement rules.

Finally, that Business Services are competing strongly in the Internal Market is a necessary but not sufficient condition for them to be competitive in an increasingly global market. Further effort to open up third country markets will in itself lead to a growing market for Business Services. It will also lead to stronger competition between European Business Services companies which under the right conditions would enable them to reach a dimension large enough to compete on the world market.

The following five actions would improve the competitive environment in which Business Service are working. They are related to: Data and information collection, quality promotion, Internal Market policies, Community trade policy and competition policy.

Action 1

To promote transparency in the supply and demand side of the market.

Measures:

▶ To improve data-collection, analyses and research on the demand and supply of Business Services by allocating more resources to this field at Community and national level. The guidelines for future work in this field, mentioned in the Report on Industrial competitiveness and Business Services (chapter 4) can be used for the initial definition of this task.

▶ To examine in detail the dynamics of Business Services, taking particular note of the role of smaller firms and their potential contributions to its future development

▶ To support dissemination of the information collected to all interested parties, while ensuring that this does not restrict or distort effective competition.

▶ To promote measures for improving quality and access to certification of Business Services in a partnership approach with the interested parties.

▶ To evaluate shortcomings in quality assessment and to support improvements.

Action 2

To create an Internal Market for Business Services

Measures:

▶ To undertake a Single market review on all possible barriers to entry in the different Business Services activities, including national regulatory and administrative barriers as well as self-regulatory professional rules.

▶ To examine the recommendations of the Business Environment Simplification Task Force ('BEST') and their implications for this sector and, in particular, to consider how the conditions under which new enterprises are launched can be improved.

▶ On the basis of the results of the above mentioned exercise, to assess together with the Member States the proportionality of identified barriers and to apply the competition rules for the Treaty with a view to abolishing all barriers which are not justifiable by reasons of public interest, security, health etc. in accordance with Article 59 of the Treaty.

▶ To contribute to the identification of best practice in the provision and promotion of Business Services in the Member States, under the Concerted Actions on Support Services for SMEs, and to develop a strategy for enhancing the visibility of Business Services, within the broader context of the promotion of support services to enterprises.

Action 3

To improve the functioning of the European public procurement market for Business Services

Measure:

▶ To take into account, in the amendments of the public procurement directives which we have announced in the Commission Communication on Public Procurement in the European Union, possibilities to make procurement procedures more flexible and allowing dialogue between purchasers and suppliers in the course of such procedures and not just in exceptional circumstances.

Action 4

To ensure that EU and national competition policies are based on the best possible knowledge of the Business Services sector

Measure:

▶ To analyse continuously the structure of the European Business Services market and to reflect the results of such analyses on Community and national competition policies.

▶ To systematically examine the impact of competition decisions concerning Business Services companies on the competitiveness of EU Industry.

Action 5

To further open up international markets to EU Business Services

Measure:

▶ To establish stronger links between the Commission and the European Business Services sector to ensure their active support to the preparation of the GATS 2000 round of negotiations.

Objective D Promotion of industrial cooperation between Business Services suppliers

As mentioned under the Objective on improving competition in the Business Services sector (point C above), legal and professional barriers can prevent access to markets, effectively closing out cooperation across borders. These barriers are not the only impediments to cooperation between Business Services companies. Lack of information of possible partners, of national conditions, linguistic and cultural knowledge are serious reasons for market fragmentation.

Faced with international competition, European Business Services companies need to explore formal and informal networks of Business Services suppliers. This would not only entail the advantage of easier access to international markets but would also open up the possibilities of supplying intersectoral systems solutions, building on a great number of specialised competencies.

The following action is proposed. It is related to EU policies on: The promotion of Business Co-operation, the Information Society, quality promotion and RDT.

Action

To support the creation of cooperative networks between Business Services suppliers

Measures:

▶ To facilitate the setting up of data-bases on cooperative networks between Business Services suppliers and to promote certification of such networks in order to create confidence in the ability of these networks.

▶ To raise the visibility of the advantages of cooperation by promoting participation in projects under the Community instruments to promote business

cooperation (BC-Net, BRE, Euro-partenariat, Interprise) and the 5th RDT framework programme.

▶ To support an improved institutional representation for the entire Business Services sector.

Objective E Promotion of Business Services

Two types of market failures exist in the EU which to a certain extent can justify public support to the development of Business Services: locational factors and the size of potential client companies. Most Business Services are concentrated in the central and urban regions of the Community, while access to Business Services in peripheral regions and for SMEs are scarce. In order to remedy this situation, the Community's structural funds policy and the SME policy have promoted the use of Business Services in various ways. New possibilities for further promotion of Business Services can be found in the financial instruments created as a follow-up to the Employment Summit in Luxembourg (the SME Guarantee Facility, the European Technology Facility and the Joint European Venture Facility), and to activities under the Integrated Programme for SMEs. However, certain evidence points to a lack of knowledge in Business Services circles to the potential of these instruments which are often not perceived as applicable to the intangible nature of investment in Business Services.

Furthermore, there exists a great diversity in the way which semi-public or public support schemes are organised and carried out in the Member States. In order to avoid wasting resources, to give maximum benefits to clients using Business Services and to avoid distortion of competition between public supported and private suppliers, greater prominence needs to be given to the services of business support agencies and their interaction with private sector suppliers of Business Services.

The following three actions proposed are related to EU policies on: Structural Funds, SMEs, the Information Society and data and information collection.

Action 1

To ensure a better geographical and regional distribution of Business Services

Measures:

▶ To identify and analyse best practices for investment in Business Services in the less favoured regions in order to rationalise and consolidate present efforts based on analyses of the needs of the regional economic structure;

▶ To further focus and systematise structural funds and other actions on Business Services, in particular by giving priorities to SME-support, IT- and training applications in the development programmes.

Action 2

To facilitate the creation of new Business Services companies and expansion of existing ones

Measures:

▶ To analyse how Business Services are effected, how Business Services will be transformed and which kind of new Business Services are likely to be created by Information Society technologies and applications (e.g. electronic commerce, virtual organisations, new types of intermediation and partnerships etc).

▶ To target (i.e. by drawing up guidelines) dissemination of information on Business Services organisations and companies in order to raise their awareness of available financial instruments and other support facilities.

Action 3

To guarantee maximum benefits from semi-public or public actions in favour of Business Services

Measure:

▶ To identify the different European models and interrelationships in the promotion of Business Services and to benchmark best practices in semi-public or public actions in favour of Business Services.

Objective F **Encouraging modernisation of public administrations**

It is not only Industry which buys Business Services. Depending on political considerations and traditions, public authorities in the Member States are to various extents acquiring Business Services for reasons similar to those of Industry: cost reductions and flexibility, higher quality and expertise, innovation in administration and organisation, higher efficiency etc. Present trends in the Member States points to a slimming down of public administrations by way of further efforts of privatisation and a growing recourse to acquisition of Business Services. Such a process could have two interlinked consequences: A more efficient public administration and as a side effect, the emergence of a bigger market for Business Services.

These interlinked objectives could be supported by the following data and information collection action:

Action

To gain better insight into the consequences of outsourcing certain public administration activities

Measure:

▶ To benchmark best practices in the Member States on the basis of indicators and a methodology to be developed.

The Business Services sector is the major economic sector with the highest growth rates in value added and employment over the last years. Their importance for the competitiveness of European enterprises and economic growth merits stronger political attention. *There are huge potentials for strengthening their role in the European economy* by putting into action policies to ameliorate their framework conditions through improving the business environment for SMEs in the sector, and by providing support to productivity improvement, job creation, competition, enterprise cooperation, public promotion and the modernisation of public administrations.

In the elaboration of a European policy on Business Services, the Commission has scrupulously respected the subsidiarity principle. All actions are proposed inside the realm of existing Community policies. They only concern tasks which cannot be sufficiently achieved by the Member States in isolation and they can therefore, by reason of the scale or effects of the proposed actions, be better achieved by the Community.

This approach naturally limits the scope of this Communication to actions of a more "soft" character. They basically concern the following three fields:

▶ an improvement of the *knowledge* on the situation of Business Services by a reinforcement of data and information collection necessary for a refinement of policy actions;

▶ raising of the *awareness of Business Services circles* on the possibility of improving their situation inside existing Community policies and *of policy makers* of the specifities of Business Services which need to be taken into account in policy formulation;

▶ the beginning of a process leading to the creation of a *true Internal Market* for Business Services.

Over time with the improvement of information on Business Services and additional Commission projects on knowledge acquisition on other services adding value to Industry, mentioned in the Report on Industrial Competitiveness and Business Services, the intention of the Commission is to further develop policy actions in a continuous process.

The Commission will periodically report on progress in this field together with an evaluation of the actions proposed in chapter 5 and propose new initiatives on Business Services and other related services adding value to Industry.

Annex 1 References

- White paper on growth, competitiveness and employment *(doc.COM(93)700, Dec 1993)*

- Commission Communication on an Industrial Competitiveness Policy for the European Union *(doc.COM(94)319 final of 14-9-1994)*

- A Confidence Pact on Employment *(doc.SEC(96)1093 of 6-5-1996)*

- An Integrated programme for SMEs and the Craft sector *(doc.COM(96)329 final of 13-7-1996)*

- The European Observatory for SMEs, Fourth Annual Report (1996), Chapter 5

- Single Market Review *(doc.COM(96)520 final of 30-10-1996)*

- First action plan for Innovation in Europe *(doc.COM(96)589 of 07-11-96)*

- Commission Communication on Europe at the forefront of the Global Information Society: Rolling Action Plan *(doc.COM(96)607 of 27-11-1996)*

- Commission Communication on Benchmarking the Competitiveness of European Industry *(doc.COM(96)463 final of 9-10-1996)*

- Commission Communication on putting Services to Work *(doc.CSE(96)6 final of 27-11-1996)*

- Commission Report on the Competitiveness of European Industry *(doc SEC(96)2121/2 of 03-03-1997)*

- Commission Communication on Commercial Communications *(doc COM(98)121 final)*

Annex 2 Basic data on Business Services

Table 1 — Basic statistics on Business Services Europe-15 (*)

	Business Services	% of Total Economy
Employment (1994)	11 635 000	8.5%
Value Added (1994) (MECU)	863 500	15.3%
Firms (1995)	2 690 130	15.0%
Exports (1993) (MECU)	31 785	2.0%
Imports (1993) (MECU)	34 107	2.0%

(*) Estimates for EUR 15 based on available data from Eurostat and OECD. Trade data are for EUR12.
Source: OECD (1996) Services: Statistics on Value Added and Employment, and EUROSTAT (1996) International Trade in Services; (1997) Statistics in Focus 1997/4, Market Services in Europe.

Table 2 — Annual average growth rates on Business Services Europe-15 (*)

Annual Growth Rates	Business Services	Manufacturing and services
Employment (1980-94)	5.5%	0.4%
Value Added (1980-94)	5.4%	1.5%
Exports (1984-93)	8.7%	5.1%
Imports (1984-93)	10.2%	5.2%

(*) Estimates for EUR 15 based on available data from EUROSTAT and OECD. Trade data are for EUR12.
Source: OECD (1996) Services: Statistics on Value Added and Employment, and EUROSTAT (1996) International Trade in Services; (1997) Statistics in Focus 1997/4, Market Services in Europe.

Table 3 — Value added: Business Service/Manufacturing

	Europe 15	United States
Business Services	15.3	19.2
Manufacturing	21.2	18.0
BS / Manufacturing	72%	106%

Source: National accounts EUROSTAT and OECD

Annex 3   Figures on Value Added and Employment

Figure 1   Gross Value Added EUR-15

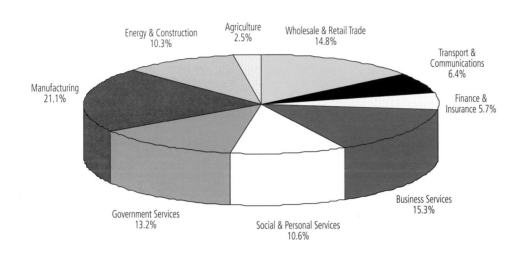

Source: Estimates for 1994 based on OECD (1996) Services: statistics on value added and employment

Figure 2   Employment EUR-15

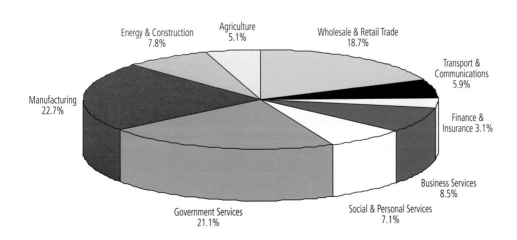

Source: Estimates for 1994 based on OECD (1996) Services: statistics on value added and employment

Annex 4   Business Services comparisons between representative European countries and the United States

	Number of Firms, 1995	Employment 1994 (thousands)	Business Services in Total Employment	Gross Value Added (*), 1994 (billions Ecu)	Business Services in Total Value Added
Austria	35 484	151	4.5%	20	11.8%
Denmark	90 742	156	6.3%	18	16.6%
Finland	31 255	125	6.5%	11	15.6%
France	427 074	1 811	8.2%	202	18.0%
Germany [1]	642 339	2 805	9.8%	220	14,2% [2]
Netherlands	88 326	496	9.3%	41 [3]	16.4%
Sweden	107 205	266	6.6%	29	17.5%
U. Kingdom	359 686	2 013 [4]	9.3% [4]	146	19.5%
Average EUR8			7.6%		16.2%
United States		12 055 [5]	10.4% [5]	1 038 [5]	19.2%

	Employment 1980-90	Annual Growth Rate 1990-94	Gross Value Added 1980-90	Annual Growth Rate (**) 1990-94
Austria		3.6%	14.6%	8.8%
Denmark	4.1%	0.6%	5.4%	2.9%
Finland	8.5%	−2.5%	8.0%	−3.1%
France	5.8%	0.3%	4.3%	3.8%
Germany [1]	4.4%	5.2%	15.1% [2]	11.1% [2]
Netherlands	6.5%	4.3%	14.7%	6.8% [3]
Sweden	7.0%	−1.5%	1.6%	1.5%
U. Kingdom		0.7% [4]	4.2%	1.0%
Average EUR8	6.0%	1.3%	8.5%	4.1%
United States	7.6%	2.1% [5]	7.8%	5.1% [5]

(*) Gross Value Added 1994, ECU in current market prices except for Denmark, United Kingdom (factor cost) and Finland and Sweden (basic values)

(**) Gross Value Added Growth Rates at constant 1990 ECU market prices except for Denmark, United Kingdom (factor cost) and Finland and Sweden (basic values)

[1] West Germany. Data on business services (employment and value added) are in the item «other business services» including auxiliary financial services and some personal services.

[2] Germany, 1993; growth rates 1990-93 and 1980-93.

[3] Netherlands, 1992; annual growth rates for 1990-92 and 1980-92

[4] Employment data for UK are estimates from OECD and Eurostat national accounts based on number of employees.

[5] United States 1993; annual growth rates for 1990-93 and 1980-93

Sources: OECD (1996) Services statistics on value added and employment (Value Added and Employment data) and Eurostat (1997) Market Services, Statistics in Focus 1997/4 (Number of Firms data)

Annex 5   Figure on the role of Business Services in the economy

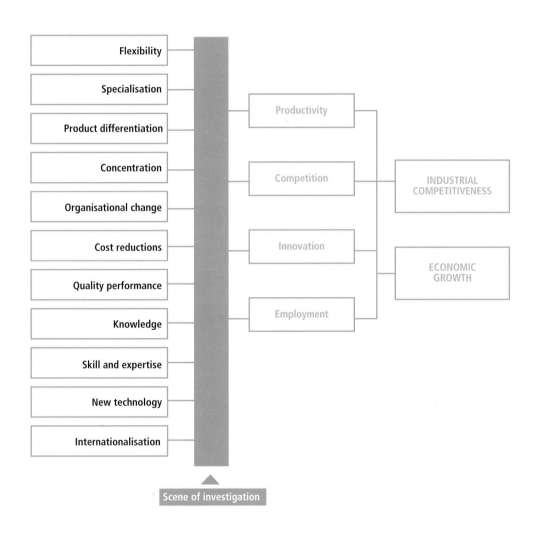

WORKING DOCUMENT OF THE COMMISSION SERVICES

Industrial Competitiveness
and Business Services
Report to the Industry Council

Table of contents

Chapter 1 | Introduction

The Industry Council of the 6-7/11/1995 invited in its Conclusions on Industrial Competitiveness and Business Services the Commission to carry out an analysis on their contribution to the competitiveness of European enterprises and job creation.

As a first step in this analysis, the Commission services have endeavoured in a stock-taking of existing statistical and analytical material with a view to identifying the gaps in our knowledge. The result of this stock-taking is the subject of the present factual report. It confirms that the level and the quality of existing information need to be seriously upgraded. Only when this has been done can solid conclusions be drawn on how to improve the framework conditions in which Business Services are working, with the overall objective of improving the competitiveness of European Industry.

It is the intention of the Commission to address this question in a future Communication. In accordance with the above-mentioned Conclusions, this Communication will also deal with the arguments for and against developing a European policy on this subject.

In the following, the present Report will deal with:

- ▶ a description of the various Business Services sectors and their general and specific characteristics;

- ▶ a preliminary analysis of the situation of Business Services, their role in the economy and their importance for a well functioning European Industry.

- ▶ statistics and their shortcomings;

- ▶ the needs for further research;

- ▶ an organisational set-up for future work;

- ▶ Conclusions with an outline of what could be the issues of the future Communication on Industrial Competitiveness and Business Services with an identification of policy issues which need detailed treatment.

| Chapter 2 | **Business Services characteristics**

A. General characteristics

Most Business Services consist of activities which are relatively new in their nature and thus not yet covered by statistical production of national statistical institutes.

They are traditionally defined in a residual way. They do not include public services (services of a general economic interest), financial services, distributive services, welfare services and household services but are classified as «other services to business». Annex 1 contains an overview of all tradable services.

Business Services are first of all characterised by their very heterogeneous nature. They are bundled together in the new European activity classification nomenclature (NACE Rev.1) according to their relations to the market i.e. the Business Service function performed for the account of the client company. They consist of 26 activities which can be grouped into the 8 subsectors mentioned below under point B.

According to the EUROSTAT publication "Business Services in Europe" from 1995, Business Services include the classes 72, 74 and 71 from section K, of the NACE Rev.1 classification. The other classes in section K, classes 70 (real estate services), 73 (research and development) as well as the subclass 74.15 (holding companies) are not included in the definition. The following table illustrates this configuration:

▶ **Definition of Business Services according to NACE Rev. 1. classification**

NACE class	Services (see details in annex 2)	Classification of Product Activities (CPA)
72	Computer and related services	72.1-6
74	Professional services	74.11, 74.12 and 74.14
74	Marketing services	74.13 and 74.4
74	Technical services	74.2, 74.3
71	Renting and leasing services	71.1, 71.21–23, 71.31-33
74	Labour recruitment and provision of personnel	74.5
74	Operational services	74.6 and 74.7
74	Other Business Services	74.81–84

The annual growth rate in value added was estimated at around 13% between 1982 and 1990. During the economic crisis in the beginning of the 1990's this growth rate fell to between 2 and 5% but has now rebounded to a growth rate of more than 10%. These figures do not include Business Services activities carried out as secondary activities within the manufacturing and other services industry. Recent estimates

(1994) based on national accounts indicate that in the manufacturing industry alone up to 33% of the employment is estimated to be due to Business Services activities.

According to the same estimates Business Services represent 10% of the total European employment and 14% of the gross value added to the economy. This means that Business Services in Europe employ around 12 million persons (1994) which created added value to the economy of more than 800 billion ECU, represented by more than 2 million enterprises. Furthermore, Business Services account for around 25-30% of EU total services exports to third countries.

Despite these impressive figures and the obvious importance of the Business Services sector in itself, *their key importance lies in their dynamic links and contribution to the competitiveness of European enterprises*, both in manufacturing industry and other Services sectors outside Business Services. They constitute an interactive relationship and mutual interdependency between suppliers and users through their intermediate inputs and through the gains in quality and innovation for their users. Business services companies enjoy expansion thanks to their market recognition and client companies, regaining profitability, generate new investment and employment.

What they have in common is that they are integrated into production, with a direct input and with strategic importance for the competitiveness of enterprises at the micro-economic level. Lower prices, higher quality and improved labour and capital productivity in Business Services have a flow-on impact on manufacturing and other services by spreading low costs to the users, by liberating resources to allocate new activities and by driving motivation for innovation.

By their nature Business Services can be performed in-house, but a continuos trend has been towards externalisation for reasons of specialisation, flexibility, cost-saving and the rising complexity of services needed by industry in an economy characterised by more recourse to knowledge-based inputs. This trend is reinforced by the emergence of new information and communication technologies and the exploitation of the possibilities opened up by the Information Society is of a particular importance to the competitiveness of Business Services.

B. The 8 main sectors of Business Services

An overview of all the activities within Business Services according to their NACE classification is found in annex 2. Since the main objective and focus of this Report is to describe and analyse the general role of Business Services as a support to Industry and its competitiveness, the 8 subsectors are only briefly described below. For a more comprehensive description reference is made to the Panorama of EU-Industry 1997.

1. Computer and related services

In the last decade, the computer services have been the fastest expanding Business Services subsector. It accounts for between 11 and 15 percent of the total turnover in Business Services and is characterised by a very high degree of dynamics, innovation, globalisation and competition. In the late 90's the subsector is renamed the Information Technology (IT) subsector constituting some of the most vital parts of the Information Society. The subsector is very important for the development of the effectiveness and competitiveness of enterprises in other sectors. Commonly, the knowledge based information technology services of the subsector is highlighted but the subsector also produces routine works.

The reasons for the rapid growth in the subsector is not only the general growth in the computer industry but also the recent trend of a high degree of externalisation compared to the externalisation in other Business Services subsectors.

The growth is reflected in high labour costs per employee. There is a high demand for qualified personnel which is reflected in the salaries.

Provisional figures suggest a high rate of internal trade within the EU and a low rate of trade with third countries. Given that most of the EU's main trading partners have opened their markets for these services, it is not immediately apparent why European service suppliers appear to be discouraged from international work. Further study is needed to establish whether market access barriers in third countries are the cause of the problems in this area.

2. Professional services

The professional services contain some of the more traditional services such as legal services, accountancy services and auditing which mainly operate on a domestic market. These services rank low in turnover and investment per employee. It has one of the lowest export shares of Business Services subsectors. With a few exceptions, less than 5% of the turnover is generated from exports to other EU countries.

Despite the fact that there is Community legislation on the mutual recognition of qualifications and, as regards the legal profession, also on the mutual recognition of authorisations to practise, the practice of the relevant activities remains to a large extent confined to national markets. This is due to a variety of factors, including remaining impediments caused by professional rules and legislation. It may, however, be expected that cross-border movements, co-operation and international competition will increase over the years, which will lead to demands for the lifting of obstacles, for instance through more convergence of the relevant rules of conduct or the development of common rules of conduct.

These characteristics are not shared by a new and emerging professional service represented by management consultancy. As explained later in the analytical part of this report, rapid technological development is putting pressure on companies to re-organise their organisational structure towards more flexible management tools. This, together with the growing importance of knowledge management in companies is opening up a new market for management consultancy which could grow at a rate similar to the market for IT services and integration of these two types of services is underway.

3. Marketing services

This subsector shows a very large volume in turnover per employee from sales of advertisement space and time sales. The turnover per employee is between 3 and 5 times higher than the national average turnover in the Business Services sector. Marketing services is one of the subsectors with the highest investment level per employee. The reduction in the cost of telecommunications, due to liberalisation and the subsequent growing use of information technology and multi-media is expected to lead to an increasing degree of specialisation in the subsector.

Due to the high level of internationalisation, direct exports are scarce. Because global marketing ser-

vices tend to set up subsidiaries, marketing services can be offered everywhere in the world. Access to the profession is unrestricted but differences in national rules and regulations on advertising are causing barriers to trade. Apart from specific advertising rules (alcohol, tobacco etc.) the context for cross-border trading companies comprises such diverse matters as contract laws, data protection laws, credit and payment rules, postal regulations and environmental regulations, voluntary industry codes and more practical matters such as language requirements. As with computer and related services, many EU trading partners have committed themselves under the General Agreement on Trade in Services (GATS) to an absence of restrictions.

4. Technical services

Technical services such as engineering consultancy, architects and quality management is one of the most important Business Services subsectors measured by the number of enterprises, number of people employed and turnover.

The subsector has in the last decades grown, partly through externalisation, partly through the emergence of new needs such as services related to quality management, environment and energy.

Exports to both EU markets and third countries are important despite a not too well functioning public procurement market in the EU and in third countries. Access to the professions are in general restricted by national regulations or professional rules based on product and service quality considerations.

5. Renting and leasing services

Both renting and leasing services are less developed in Europe than in the USA and the markets are not yet fully matured for these services. It is one of the minor Business Services subsectors in terms of volume and in terms of employment it is even smaller. The subsector is characterised by large investments which act as an entry barrier as opposed to other subsectors. As a consequence, the gross value added per employee is one of the highest among the Business Services sectors.

Trade between EU countries is well developed. The main regulatory trade barrier is major differences between Member Sates with respect to accounting rules. Furthermore, differences in VAT and excise duties are causing rental and leasing companies to charge different prices in different Member States, leading to intransparencies in the market. Exports to third countries are not significant with the exception of a growing market in the Eastern European countries.

6. Labour recruitment and provision of personnel

This subsector has shown a considerable growth and an increasing importance for the economy in the last years, caused by a growing use of temporary employment in order to increase the flexibility of enterprises and thus their competitiveness. Particularly the larger enterprises in this subsector have diversified into a sophisticated service industry providing instruments for labour management, computer software services, business information, financial services, security, cleaning and language services. Since temporary workers often find permanent employment through their temporary assignment, the industry has also turned into personnel recruitment advisors.

Cross border activity takes place only on a very small scale. Temporary work businesses wishing to operate in foreign countries generally do this by starting a local branch or by buying into a local company.

The subsector is undergoing a deregulation and liberalisation process in most of the Member States where the services were undertaken by the public sector.

In countries with a liberal regulatory regime, a shortage of qualified temporary personnel has proven an obstacle to growth. This shows the importance of training provided by an increasing number of temporary work business and increasing importance of quality assurance.

7. Operational services

The industrial cleaning part of this subsector is one of the economically most important Business Services sectors both in terms of employment and in turnover (more than 2 million mainly part-time workers and a turnover of above 22 billion). A wide range of other operational support services, such as security, catering, building maintenance, waste collection etc. has been incorporated into services offered by industrial cleaning services. Take-overs and mergers, both horizontally and vertically, are frequent and the number of bigger companies are on the rise.

Cross border provision of services is rare and limited to neighbouring regions or specific contracts. The bigger companies usually operate via a network of local agencies.

The main function of the subsector is not related to the productive aspects of enterprises and their importance in enhancing the competitiveness of industry is limited. The major importance of the subsector is related to its employment creation.

In most countries, operational services except security services are not subject to entry barriers, although voluntary codes of conduct and certification of qualifications lead to a certain auto-limitation. A number of restrictive national regulations impact negatively on the development of the services and, even in the absence of direct discrimination, on cross-border activity in the Internal Market. Labour costs account for the main part of companies turnover and operational services are therefore highly sensitive to social legislation such as recruitment and dismissal regulations, overtime restrictions and rules on transfer of undertakings.

8. Other Business Services

The residual of Business Services comprises activities as diverse as photography, bill collecting, fashion design and interior decoration, trade fairs and congress activities etc. Apart from trade fairs and exhibitions their importance for industrial competitiveness is limited and common traits are difficult to find. However entry barriers and barriers to cross border trade are scarce.

| Chapter 3 | **Preliminary analysis of the situation of Business Services** | 3 |

A. Dynamic links to Industry

Service sector activities currently correspond, on average, to two thirds of economic activity in EU Member States (services account for 63% of total EU value-added) and appear to be increasingly important in a large number of areas. The convergence and interdependence between manufacturing and services is growing and the services element now often tends to outweigh the manufacturing element in the final product rather than the other way around. This is all the more true for Business Services.

Nevertheless, the exact interaction between Business Services and Industry currently still needs to be understood in detail. Apart from the statistical problems mentioned in the following chapter, one of the difficulties concerning information on supply and demand of Business Services is a lack of disaggregation between the different services sectors. Often Business Services are treated together with financial services and/or distributive trade and/or household services. For these reasons, some of the information below refers to a wider group of services used by industry where Business Services are following the general trends in services.

It is becoming increasingly well understood that a great number of the cost pressures on Industry are generated not within manufacturing, but in the service sectors. These "input services" to manufacturing are in many cases not competitive in Europe. The resulting negative downstream externalities, effectively reduce the competitiveness of Europe's manufacturing industry. The increased cost of inputs, by necessity, increases the cost of the final product, which causes lower demand for a particular product and in turn reduces the willingness to invest in this sector.

B. Sectors of greatest strategic importance

All Business Services impact Industry, but they are not all equally important to industrial competitiveness. Recent analyses have identified the sectors believed to be of greatest strategic importance to Industry (by reducing costs or by adding value to industries' activities) as well as a model that gives an indication of possible synergy effects between Business Services subsectors. In this context «strategic» has been defined as such Business Services sectors having general applicability to industrial sectors as well as being an integral part of the production chain. The resulting five Business Services sectors were also identified by Industry as having the greatest strategic importance for their operations and hence their competitiveness:

▶ Management consultancy

▶ ICT Services

▶ Engineering and quality control

▶ Advertising and Marketing

▶ Legal and Accounting

When one looks at the clusters and synergies in the Business Services sector, they are characterised by strong synergies between subsectors and activities, while relations with other activities carried out by the same companies are marginal.

This indicates that although analyses of all Business Services Sectors should continue, future work should be concentrated on those sectors with the strongest synergy effects and impact on industrial and in particular on SMEs' competitiveness.

▶ **Map of Business Services subsectors. Relations and synergy possibilities**

Source: Prof. Luis Rubalcaba, University of Madrid

C. Reasons for growth

1. Outsourcing

One of the main reasons for the dramatic growth in services and especially in Business Services over the last decade is that functions which were previously performed inside manufacturing industries are now outsourced to the service sector. Here an important causality takes place: the demand by Industry dictates high performance in the delivery and content of services which means that services have to conform to requirements in the fields of standardisation, norms and quality. This leads to greater demand by services for Industry-delivered technology which makes it possible to provide the service with the required specifications. The resulting virtuous cycle drives growth and creates employment provided that obstacles in the form of negative framework conditions are removed by policy makers and industry itself.

On the enterprise side the current trend towards externalisation is gathering momentum and is the consequence of two main factors:

- A growing need for increased effectiveness, quality, expertise and specialisation;

- A shift in company strategies to lower costs, «lean production and management», higher flexibility, focus on core value added activities and most critical business areas, while outsourcing all other services.

The outsourcing phenomenon was at a first stage clearly linked to computer technology. From the 1990's, with the introduction of digitalisation in networks, integrating voice, data and images, links between computers and telecommunications became strong. This in turn opened up a number of business opportunities and possibilities related to the externalisation of functions and to the incorporation of products and services linked to communications technologies in Business Services companies. Since this convergence process began, it is increasingly difficult for Business Services companies to stay competitive if they are not at the forefront of this process.

2. Globalisation

At macro-economic level, the term "globalisation" refers to the growing integration of national economies through trade and foreign direct investment and then to the emergence of new patterns in the international transfer of products and knowledge. Business Services such as ICT services are an essential element in the globalisation of Industry, which would not be conceivable without these services.

As to the globalisation of Business Services themselves, trade and foreign direct investment in the field of advanced Business Services is essentially transfer of knowledge. By capital mobility and international communications improvement through IT technology, national borders have become more permeable to Business Services activity.

Globalisation of Business Services is characterised by three main routes: international trade, international direct investment and international co-operation agreements. This phenomenon is driven by a number of economic, political and technological forces, which include: higher fixed costs and a resulting need to exploit economies of scale; competitive pressures which make it necessary to take advantage of international cost differentials; access to markets; by addressing to different targets and finally the need for flexibility caused by rapidly changing markets.

Consequently globalisation of Business Services is the result of their innovative response as they exploit opportunities and adapt to changes in their technological and institutional environment. The factors shaping globalisation of Business Services can be divided into four groups, many of which are inter-linked:

- Firm behaviour, as strategic-initiative behaviour, exploitation of competitive advantages;

- Technology-related factors: declining communication costs, increasing customisation, increasing importance of customer-oriented services;

- Macro-economic factors, as availability of key knowledge factors, productivity differentials, fluctuations in exchange rates;

- Government policies: promotion of regional integration, intellectual property rights, inward investment incentives, R&D technology, small firms and related industry policies.

Business Services themselves can have different strategies to internationalise their operations. With the decline in communications and transport costs, the globalisation of activities and the need to locate in the three strategically important areas of world economic activity, growth and investment (North America, Europe, Asia) Business Services firms can go off-shore to locate in areas of efficient low cost delivery, where there are strong externalities and agglomeration economies to encourage location, such as a good supply of highly trained and experienced labour, efficient communications and transport links, the appropriate time zone location and other externalities. Alternatively, Business Services firms may re-locate part of their operations in the same region or country to be close to their internationalising clients, following the same location pattern as for example parts producers in the automobile industry.

The liberalisation of international trade in services offers considerable benefits to the suppliers of business services and, by increasing competition within the Community itself, could have a favourable impact on the costs to the rest of industry of these services. Under the General Agreement on Trade in Services (GATS), countries make specific binding commitments on sectors ranging from accountancy services to computer services and marketing, thereby entitling EU service suppliers to non-discriminatory market access and national treatment in a diverse range of business services. Commitments tend to be particularly liberal in areas away from the regulated professions. The EU itself has similarly made a broad range of commitments in the business services area. The challenge is to ensure that EU service providers take full advantage of these legally enforceable commitments. Where it is found that markets are not as open as they should be, the barriers to trade should be clearly identified so that appropriate action can be taken, if necessary through the WTO's dispute settlement procedure, in order to remedy the situation.

Even so, some important constraints on globalisation of Business Services come to light:

- Differences between national markets and the inherent needs of their consumers have not disappeared.

- The costs of integrating a global value chain, such as freight and duty, telecommunications and travel, and the cost of time delays can be significant impediments to exports of Business Services.

Services with significant direct trade potential represent half of all services and 30% of the economy as a whole. Yet the share of European service exports has remained stable at 20% of total trade, since 1980, whilst that of European service imports has grown to 18% of total trade. Case in point is the Business Service Sector which has seen the external trade surplus shrink from 4 billion ECU in the 1980's to less than 1 billion ECU in the 1990's. This is reason for concern, given that part of European goods imports are caused by lack of natural resources in Europe, while this is not true for Business Services with their high value added content. Clearly there is potential for further service development on the European market, but European service providers are not able to realise the opportunities.

3. The impact of new technology on services

Business Services are a key factor for technological innovation and industrial competitiveness as they directly and indirectly affect the value chain up- and downstream.

Although services output has traditionally been consumed when produced, underscoring the intrinsic, intangible nature of many service sectors, technological development is constantly enhancing the tradability of services.

Information and Communication Technologies (ICT), allow for increased tradability of service activities, particularly those which have been most constrained by the geographical (or time) proximity of production and consumption. By bringing in a space or time/storage dimension, ICT makes it possible to separate production from consumption in a large number of such activities. A good example is the many new online data services.

These new technologies are likely to further open up many service activities, which will increase their domestic and international tradability. Technological change increases the content of services in manufacturing output. ICTs are in effect making services more like manufacturing, leading to a further convergence of industrial and service activities which particularly applies to Business Services.

This is why there is a need to build a strong technological base for innovation in services. Creation and innovation in services can only be sustained if

Europe has a strong base in the supporting information and communications technology. The current situation though is very unbalanced, with such technology largely being imported from the US rather than being developed in Europe. In the short run this may suffice to assist in take-up of current best practice. However, in the longer run, Europe will increasingly miss «first mover advantage» in new markets if it does not significantly contribute to the development of key technologies and a solid skills base for new services. Community RTD programmes could further develop their catalytic role in this respect, while other programmes provide training in the use of such new technologies.

4. Shift in organisational structure

The productivity gains made from technological innovation have during the past few decades had the tendency to diminish the relative and absolute demand for labour (cf. below in employment section). However, one should keep in mind that all technological innovations pass through several stages: The full economic benefits as well as the employment creating potential is not realised during the first stage. *These take place, after the organisational aspects (i.e.: how the work is divided; how the technology is used; how information is managed) have been adapted to the new situation.* Historically, organisational innovation has lagged behind product and process innovations. The general issue is that new technology is inherently applied to an organisational model which was developed for the preceding technology. Therefore, product market developments require complimentary developments in the internal structure of organisations. For example, advances in micro electronics brought about the concept of quality checks integrated in the production process (TQM), rather than final product quality control.

Nevertheless, it is not enough to analyse the extent to which the latest management trends are applied in companies, industrial sectors and countries. *A viable organisation is one which has change and flexibility engraved in its structure.* The ability to change is determinant, not the name of the latest trend. Organisations need to acquire the ability to evaluate and embrace improvements in the organisational field as they have already been attempting to do in the areas of new technologies and products. Business Services give industry the ability to respond more adequately to such needs.

With the increasing «dematerialisation» of value added and the growing importance of services, enhanced by the rising application of ICT, organisational flexibility becomes a necessary precondition for companies to offer new services. Advanced information technologies accelerate the rate at which service providers are able to offer new products. These new intangible products necessitate changes in the way in which information is handled within organisations.

Equally changes in internal structures may result in new services being created. Even manufactured products, which are now being created, differentiate themselves not essentially by their physical appearance, but by the non-tangible service component which they include. An example of this may be automobiles where the non-tangible product content may include such services as: free road-side assistance, free maintenance services, reverse GPS systems that make it possible to locate the vehicle if it is stolen, free help-desk phone-number, magazines, etc. Of equal importance is the integration of business services into other service sectors. The offering of «bundles» of services

on the market is a phenomenon of rapidly growing economic significance.

D. Employment impact of services

It is well established that services employment has become essential for overall employment growth, seeing that manufacturing employment has fallen substantially since early 1990's.

As mentioned earlier, the Information Society is pervading and modifying most aspects of economic, industrial and social life. It is obvious that ICT are bringing productivity gains, not only to industry, but increasingly in administrations and in particular the service sector. Greater use of ICT intensifies global competition which in turn should have a positive impact on employment. Currently ICT is creating jobs directly in the new service industries (multimedia, consultancy), as well as indirectly due to the trickle-down effect of greater purchasing power resulting from productivity gains. This is why many now turn towards the Business Services sector looking for an additional source of employment, replacing redundant manufacturing jobs.

▶ **Decline in manufacturing employment 1990 to 1995**

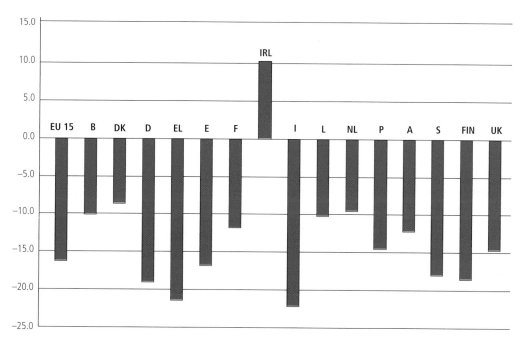

Source: Eurostat 1997, D including new länder, Denmark only 1993 data

The precise job creating potential of the Business Services sector and of advanced Business Services in particular can not currently be adequately quantified due to the lack of reliable statistical and analytical data. For, although Business Services represent an economic sector with high economic growth, indications are that it has as of yet failed to translate itself into job creation of a magnitude that can compensate for the losses in other economic sectors.

The challenge is that seemingly new jobs are created only gradually and not in the same sectors as those where jobs are being displaced resulting in the observed high levels of structural unemployment in Europe. Consequently, one needs to be cautious in making employment forecasts, but it is clear that there is an urgent need for skills retraining.

However, the following, general facts and figures seem to be consistent and robust. For the sectors which showed the most substantial employment growth in the EU, during the period 1970-93, market services witnessed above average employment growth. This pattern is more or less equivalent to the one observed in the US.

- Data network services: 13% growth in 1995

- Voice network services: 8% growth in 1995

- Finland experienced a 4% growth in employment for the entire telecommunications cluster (including equipment manufacturing) over the period 1987-93, while total employment fell by 16%.

- GSM telecommunications liberalization created 30 000 jobs in Germany.

- Comparative data of EU-4 (D, F, IT, SP), the US and Japan for the time-span 1980 to 1990 show that while market services created jobs, both agriculture and manufacturing lost jobs or remained stagnant.

For both the US and Japan the employment gains made in the market service sector outweighed the losses made in the other two sectors. Of the three, Europe recorded the lowest job creation in market ser-

---

▶ **Net Jobs created (per 100 working age population) 1980 to 1990**

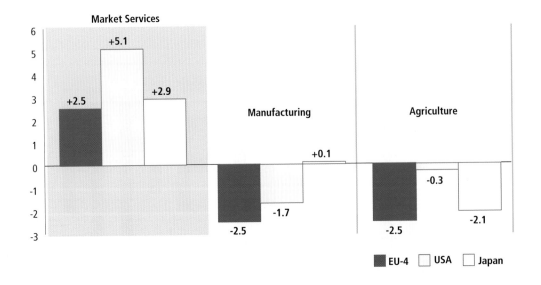

Source: Eurostat & DGIII

vices while experiencing the greatest losses in manufacturing and agriculture. As a result, losses in Europe considerably outweighed European increases. Especially private employment creation is suffering as it is more vulnerable to macro-economic developments.

Business Services, as a result of the increased tradability and an increased outsourcing of intermediate input together with growing labour market flexibility have become much more dependent on cyclical swings of the economy. As an increasing number of service activities are becoming liberalised or opened up to international competition, these sectors are likely to become much more responsive to macro-economic developments.

The hope is that increased tradability will raise productivity as Business Services markets are affected by competitive pressures. This will entail lower prices for Business Services, which in turn raises demand for Business Services. Viewed at an aggregate level, it will result in more economic activity leading to higher real incomes and demand. The rise in aggregate demand will subsequently encourage new investment in the economy as a whole and create new employment opportunities.

As a result, a dynamic and thriving Business Services sector is important not only as a creator of employment in its own right. *The real issue is their added value input to manufacturing industry with its positive effects on employment, competitiveness and growth in Industry.*

E. Measurement of productivity

The most serious problem is the present inability to clearly account for differences in quality and thereby measure real output in the services area in general and particularly in the Business Services. Some progress in this field - e.g. with a more harmonised breakdown into prices and volumes - will be needed in the framework of the Pact on Stability and Growth which takes up the real GDP figures.

Certainly turnover per employee is not an adequate measure. National variations in labour costs, sunk costs and labour-capital substitution levels are just one problematic issue. The choice which enterprises make in this respect often decides on the level of profitability of each one.

Profitability is a function of Total Factor Productivity (TFP), which takes the productivity of all factors of investment into account. TFP becomes especially important in the context of Business Services. These often have considerable capital investments which need to be amortised. Furthermore, TFP needs to be seen in context: in low productivity countries, costs are also lower for certain of the factors and therefore TFP may well be equivalent to high productivity countries. One will use more of the abundant (and cheap) resources. This has direct implications for policy formulation in such areas as taxation, structural policy, pay equalisation etc. For divergent cases a different policy instrument mix may need to be used in order to achieve a similar result.

In any case, it is of prime importance to improve the ability to measure productivity of Business Services (and other services) in order to underpin arguments that liberalisation and regulatory reform will raise productivity as Business Services markets are affected by competitive pressures, cf. below under generic obstacles to enhanced competitiveness of Business Services.

F. Business Services and Structural Policies

Business Services and in particular advanced Business Services are often concentrated in the more prosperous and central regions of the Community. Recent studies carried out by the Commission Services have given two main reasons for the concentration of Business Services in the more economically advanced regions:

- From the demand point of view, clients require strong interaction with the supplier which often demands face to face meetings not easily replaced by even the most modern IT applications;

- From the supply point of view, Business Services are concentrating in areas where flows of national and international activities are most intensive and where qualified human resources are available.

Regional and social policies have over the years been actively involved in promoting the establishment of Business Services in particular in the Objective 1 regions, in order to produce convergence effects in these regions. The arrival of new activities carries on technological and capital import, producing a significant economic output with a flow-on effect on total factor productivity in the region. Business Services activities help to promote regional specialisation, exploring regional comparative advantages and they support the innovation possibilities of enterprises, reinforcing a competitive environment and adaptation to industrial changes. Coupled with training schemes in Business Services activities co-financed by the European Social Fund, the development of these types of services can have a major impact on regional development, attracting new enterprises and economic activity in general.

G. Generic obstacles to enhanced competitiveness of Business Services

As mentioned in the Commission Report on the Competitiveness of European Industry from 1996, the most important obstacle to enhanced competitiveness of Business Services is represented by *national market access restrictions*. These are barriers for the creation of pan-European Business Services. As a result, a high degree of market fragmentation can be observed among European Business Services, which tend to retain a national identity.

The legacy of national orientation and the small company size of European Business Services is reflected in the difficulty of national companies to set up cross-border operations. This legacy is amplified by severe obstacles to Internal Market integration, such as heavy national legislation, taxation, company law, access to information and advice on cross-border opportunities, cultural aspects, etc. On the contrary, foreign companies especially from the United States have established themselves on European Union markets thanks to their ability to operate cross-border on the basis of an integrated network of national subsidiaries.

For those professions for which public interest protection has led to the requirement that a specific qualification be obtained in order to practise, mutual recognition (or harmonisation) of professional qualifications is necessary to guarantee market access across different national markets. Currently, qualifications are still obtained at national level and under the control of local corporatist organisations and mutual recognition is not fully effective.

National regulations in Business Services are dictated by safety or consumer protection requirements, as well as market control and quality objectives where restrictive national leglisation can hinder the development of Business Services and their international expansion. *Regimes of self-regulation* by governing bodies may also translate into anti-competitive practices, such as fixing prices or other practices of market control. These market access restrictions lead to low relative productivity and high relative prices in the Business Services sector. It is in fact perceived (with the inherent measurement problems mentioned above under point E) that in the 1980's productivity growth in this services sector has been lower than in manufacturing. As these inefficiencies are transmitted along the value chain they also cause low levels of growth and innovation in other sectors of the economy, which depresses European industries ability to compete within the EU as well as on non-EU markets.

Furthermore, both delays in the transposition of Directives and difficulties in harmonisation of regulatory regimes imply inefficient public procurement policies which translate into high costs and poor standards in some countries.

Finally, in most Member States *public or semi-public organisations* offer subsidised Business Services similar to those provided by private sector players. This can in certain cases and under certain conditions lead to a distortion of competition. It is thus necessary to undertake an analysis on where public support covers real market failures, where public support can act as a one-stop-shop facilitating enterprises identification of the best suited private Business Service (usually of importance to SME's) and where public support acts as a genuine barrier for competition between Business Services suppliers.

The forthcoming Communication on Industrial Competitiveness and Business Services will analyse the above-mentioned questions in more detail, also taking into account the results of the Third Concerted Action - SMEs and Business Services - organised by the Commission under the framework of the Integrated Programme. Where appropriate, it will propose solutions to the problems.

One of the major problems related to the official statistical production is the clear unbalance between the statistical coverage of, on the one side, agriculture and manufacturing and on the other side, service industries. In a situation where services create more than two-thirds of the GDP of the EU Member States, it is evident that steps have to be taken to remedy the lack of statistical coverage.

The traditional service industries such as distributive trade, hotels, restaurants and transport are in most EU Member States covered by statistics on the «physical output» (functional statistics in the EUROSTAT terminology) such as number of nights spent or ton/kilometres. For Business Services the situation is more complicated for three reasons:

Firstly, because of their intangible or intellectual content, common input-output variables are imprecise. A new methodology and a new set of indicators must be established in order to measure productivity and competitiveness of Business Services.

Secondly, comparisons between EU Member States are hampered by an uneven geographical statistical coverage and different levels of aggregation of services sectors.

Thirdly, many Business Services are in new or emerging activities which are not yet reflected in national account registers.

In order to cope with these problems, EUROSTAT and national statistical institutes have lately improved their co-operation in this field in accordance with the Commission Decision 97/281/EC on the role of EUROSTAT as regards the production of Community statistics. The following will describe the actual state of play and attempt to define what are the future needs for improved Business Services statistics.

A. The existing EU framework for Business Services statistics

The EU framework for statistics on Business Services, understood as the legal basis for carrying out data collection and production of statistical output on a harmonised basis, has been considerably strengthened in the last couple of years. However, the results of this strengthening will not be immediately available and it will still be some time before profound analyses of the situation of Business Services, based on raw data, will be available. The legal framework can be described under the following four points:

1. The revision of the Statistical Classification of Economic Activities in the European Community (NACE Rev. 1) was adopted in 1993 (Council Regulation (EEC) n° 761/93 of 24 March 1993) and put into force in the Member States. This new activity classification secures, at a certain level of aggregation (4 digits), a harmonised nomenclature to be used in all Member States.

   One of the achievements with the introduction of NACE Rev. 1 - besides the comparability of business structures across Member States - is the expansion of the number of activity classes within Business Services. In view of the rapid developments and dynamics within the Business Services, this new and enlarged nomenclature for Business Services, particularly for the information technology related services, is of importance for detailed sector analysis.

2. A regulation on the creation of statistical business registers in all the Member States (Council Regulation (EEC) n° 2186/93 of 22 July 1993 on Community co-ordination in drawing up business registers for statistical purposes) entered into force in the Member States in 1993.

   The regulation foresees the building up of statistical business registers with a total sectoral coverage which in many countries has not been the case until now. Especially the service sectors - and in particular Business Services - have not yet been fully included in the existing business registers and much more work needs to be done in this field in the majority of Member States. Partly due to the prominence of micro enterprises within the Business Services and the dynamics reflected in a large number of births and deaths of enterprises in the sector, the statistical surveying is hampered without a business register with total coverage relating to activity and size of enterprise.

3. A regulation on structural business statistics (Council Regulation (EEC, EURATOM) n° 58/97 of 20 December 1996 concerning structural business statistics) entered into force in the Member States in February 1997.

   The regulation defines a number of characteristics to be surveyed for all market sectors, including Business Services. The regulation defines 11 variables, mainly accounting variables such as turnover, profit and loss account, value added at factor costs etc., for which information on a harmonised basis shall be transmitted to the Commission from the statistical year 1995 onwards.

4. Finally, a draft regulation on short term business statistics has been prepared by EUROSTAT. This regulation contains no general characteristics to be covered by all market sectors. In the initial stage the regulation will concentrate on manufacturing, construction and retail trade for which a whole set of indicators shall be collected by the Member Sates. For other services, including Business Services, the regulation provides the indications for the carrying out of pilot surveys for a transitional period of 5 years.

B. A new, supplementary approach

In an attempt to get faster results and as a complement to the existing statistical legal framework with relevance to Business Services, EUROSTAT has, in collaboration with most of the national statistical institutes, conducted a pilot survey based on a limited number of Business Services enterprises in Europe. This study (Business Services in Europe, 1995) provides a unique overview of the Business Services sector. However, because of the non-mandatory character of the pilot survey and as a consequence of inadequate registers in most of the Member States, the data collection does not always permit comparisons between Member States.

On the basis of the experience with this pilot survey, a small task force was set up by EUROSTAT and some national statistical institutes in 1995 in order to find a new approach to statistics on Business Services. Focus is more oriented towards user needs (enterprises, branch organisations and policy makers) more than on an orientation towards the needs of the national accounts and balance of payments, which are thought of being largely satisfied by the basic enterprise data in the Regulation on business registers. It was decided to carry out detailed branch studies in a small number of Member states and not a harmonised survey in all Member States which would have been too costly and time-consuming.

The result of the work of the task force was the launching of 4 pilot studies within Business Services: Information Technology Services, Labour Recruitment and Provision of Personnel, Industrial Cleaning and Engineering Services with a common core of variables enabling comparative analysis across activity classes. The result of the pilot studies will be available in 1997 and 1998 and new pilot studies in other Business Services sectors are foreseen.

C. Future needs for Business Services statistics

What is needed in the future is a comprehensive approach. The new structural business regulation, mentioned above, will imply a considerable improvement in the statistical coverage of the Business Services sector. For a number of variables, it will be possible to carry out comparative analyses of Business Services across the EU at a relatively detailed level. However, as the regulation mainly satisfies needs for macro-economic analyses, a further development of the statistics on Business Services is still needed in line with what is described in the previous section on the new, supplementary approach.

This approach is not only expected to lead to a better insight into the surveyed activities. It will also form the basis for the development of new ideas and experiences on the methodology of data collection and will raise the level of knowledge concerning which subjects and indicators are the most important for understanding the performance of Business Services. Without this knowledge it is not possible to indicate how to improve the performance of Business Services with the general objective of improving the competitiveness of industry. In order to meet the increasing needs of a wide range of users, the ultimate goal is to develop statistics on Business Services in such a way that enterprises and other economic operators can have a solid foundation for policy decisions and future investment.

In the following, the most important domains which need to be analysed in the future and the indicators determining the performance of Business Services will be treated as a first step in a more long term process (cf. below under chapter 5). Attention is drawn to the fact that collection of these new data at company level should not lead to administrative burdens on enterprises. They will be compensated by a considerable alleviation of data collection at company level following the growing recourse to national business registers, (cf. above under the new legal framework for Business Services statistics). Furthermore, enterprises themselves have an interest in obtaining information based on micro-economic level data and will thus be motivated for participating in types of surveys which, contrary to the previous situation, do not mainly satisfy government administrative needs for macro-economic analyses.

As is it the case in the existing EU legal framework on data collection and production of statistical output, confidentiality of the disaggregate data at company level must be secured. Access for individual companies to data which permit the identification of competitors and their prices, services produced and sold, market share, human and capital investment, etc., could lead to anti-competitive practices and market distortions. It is thus important to ensure an appropriate level of aggregation of the information made available to enterprises which at the same time is of sufficient relevance to help companies identifying new policies and possibilities in the market.

1. Dynamics of the Business Services Sector

This subject does not only concern the determination of traditional performance indicators such as growth in share of gross value added or employment. Special attention should be paid to enterprise demographic data like births, deaths or growth of the individual enterprises over a time period. Preliminary indicators are that annual real births of Business Services enterprises is larger than in any other sector of the economy.

2. Employment

It is a widespread view that the Business Services sector holds one of the keys to an important rise in employment. Since job creation forms part of the competitiveness issue in the sense that the high rate of unemployment is the most serious waste of resources in the European economy, it is necessary to know more about the job creation process in the relations between industry and Business Services. It is, however, not sufficient to rely on statistical information on the number of persons employed. More detailed information on the qualifications and skills of the employed is essential in order to determine the needs for further education and training in this field.

Preliminary investigations show that the need for a continuous upgrading of skills is one of the most important parameters in the competitiveness of Business Services. This is in particular the case in the knowledge based services such as ICT, engineering and quality assurance. Especially information about the educational level and orientation of the employees and managers as well as ongoing training activities and subjects should be considered as having priority in the collection of statistics on Business Services in the years to come.

3. Globalisation

Information on traditional variables such as imports and exports need to be supplemented by nationality of ownership and cross border relations including figures on Foreign Direct Investment. This last subject seems to be of an increasing importance in the form of joint ventures, licensing agreements and other forms of co-operation across the national borders through formal or informal networks. Furthermore, cross-border flows are likely to expand dramatically with the introduction of the euro.

4. Product information

It is not sufficient to know the total turnover of for instance the IT-services. It is necessary to understand the detailed breakdown of turnover by the different categories of the IT-services, i.e. the part of the turnover of the sector which derives from selling services such as education, compared to the selling of software or the differentiation between selling services and hardware. In the long term, price statistics for the sector need to be elaborated. This constitutes a main problem since rapid technological development, i.a. in computer services poses difficulties in the measuring of price/quality ratios. The future challenge is the elaboration of a new measuring methodology.

5. Innovation

A common trait within most of the Business Services sector and particularly in the knowledge based activities is an ongoing intensive innovation process. Furthermore, new technologies, concentrated around the information and communication technology sector lead to the emergence of new types of services. As a consequence, the services sector, including Business Services, has been included in the second Community Innovation Survey which was designed in the beginning of 1997. The results and methodological experiences from this survey, together with results from the above-mentioned pilot survey on Information Technology Services will form the basis for further insight and identification of methods of measurement of the innovation process and its consequences for productivity and competitiveness of Business Services.

6. Supply and demand interaction

Collection of data has until now mainly been concentrated on the supply side of Business Services. In order to really understand the development of Business Services and their contribution to the competitiveness of other economic sectors it is important to measure the outsourcing process. Ongoing pilot projects and other analytical work should therefore be extended to include the demand side of Business Services. This could furthermore contribute to solving inherent measurement problems concerning the advantages to companies of employing Business Services such as IT-services. Only the customers are able to assess the productivity of Business Services since they have an obvious interest in assessing the relations between input and output of applied Business Services.

7. The Information Society

Information Technology Services are in the centre of the Information Society, together with telecommunications, audio-visual and information technology manufacturing. The elaboration of statistics on the Information Society activities does not necessarily mean the collection of new characteristics. A first approach to Information Society statistics could be a different aggregation of already existing information. Because of its political importance work in this field is going on in most of the Member States. One possibility is to cluster Information Society activities around a complex consisting of development, production and distribution of:

- Industries operating the systems: Telecommunications, data-processing services, the technical operation of the systems;

- Equipment: Industries producing or distributing equipment for production or consumption of IT commodities and construction of the network;

- Systems and services: service information and content production: Industries producing the services and information products for the network and some closely related industries;

Classification in this field goes beyond the scope of this report but since services in the Information and Communications Technology complex are both horizontal and vertical elements in Business Services, new common delimitations are important in order to compare Business Services activities between the Member States.

8. The regional dimension

In order to integrate a regional dimension in the statistical effort and for structural policy to effectively target business services, a clear understanding of the dynamics that influence the regional geography of Business Services is needed. Thus, statistics should be collected at the most detailed level of geographical disaggregation and, in any case, at no less than NUTS II level.

> The above-mentioned approach should be considered as a first step for further reflections in this field before the elaboration of a more comprehensive strategy for establishing statistics in the Business Services sector in close co-operation between EUROSTAT and other Commission services, national statistical institutes, the main branch organisations and industry itself. Furthermore, serious consideration should be given to the viability of the narrow definition of Business Services as reflected in the NACE code. *With the emergence of many new types of services and with the growing understanding of the interaction between manufacturing and services, the present definition of Business Services could prove too limited to accurately reflect which services are the most important in the added value process in Industry.* As indicated below under chapter 6, a new definition and methodology concerning Industry Value Added Services might prove appropriate in the search for the best ways of supporting Industry and its competitiveness.

Chapter 5 | Research on Business Services

As mentioned in the introduction, very little and scattered literature on Business Services exists. Apart from the gaps in statistical data which have been defined above, there is a clear need for profound analyses and research into the situation of Business Services in order to identify possible policy measures at regional, national and Community level.

With a view to the preparation of the future Commission Communication on Industrial Competitiveness and Business Services, a number of actions have already been initiated and plans for further research into this field are taking shape.

A. Ongoing activities

A comprehensive report which will further enhance and deepen the understanding of the dynamics and other issues highlighted in chapter 3 above is under elaboration. The work is expected to be accomplished by the end of 1998 and will thus constitute an important analytical basis for the Communication.

In co-operation with the OECD, the Commission is furthermore co-financing an analysis on information technology, organisational change and productivity in an international perspective, which has specific relevance for the development of existing and new advanced Business Services; Both manufacturing and Service companies are analysed. This study will enable better understanding of the relationship between information technology, organisational structure and productivity of companies by developing accurate methods of measures, models of the principal phenomena and field based observation, utilising samples from firms in the USA, Europe and Japan. Apart from

making international comparisons possible, it would also lead to a better understanding on how new technology affects the content of Business Services and the basic co-ordination processes within and between Business Service providers and their clients and to find a complementary relation between information technology deployment and organisational architecture.

Finally, under the specific programme on «Targeted Socio-Economic Research» (TSER), a number of research projects concerning Business Services have been launched. These projects intend, for example, to shed more light on the impact of Business Services on innovation and regional development. One of these research networks has just concluded its final report, investigating and highlighting the strategic role of knowledge-intensive services for the transmission and application of technical and management innovation.

B. Planned activities

Depending on available resources, more sector specific analyses within Business Services and their relations to manufacturing, agriculture and other services, geographical coverage and specific scopes such as outsourcing, globalisation, employment etc. is necessary since conditions vary within the different sectors. A matrix of the possible dimensions in such new studies and the possible permutations is shown in annex 3.

It is furthermore the intention to undertake benchmarking in selected strategic sectors. The feasibility of benchmarking these areas depends on progress in the above-mentioned statistical and analytical fields, because of the necessity to develop physical performance indicators for measuring best practices.

EU's main competitors, the USA and Japan, possess institutional frameworks which are closely monitoring and analysing the situation of all tradable services and their contribution to the economy. In the USA this work is undertaken by Congressional and Presidential subcommittees in close co-operation with relevant government and state administrations. In Japan, the MITI has created a specific centre for economic analyses of the service sector.

A lack of systematic and continuous monitoring and analyses of the services sector could seriously hamper Europe's possibility of catching new emerging services markets and at the same time entail the risk that European services companies on the EU market are losing out to outside competition, simply because of too little knowledge on strengths and weaknesses of European services companies. This is particularly serious in the Business Services sector because of its growing tradability.

The Commission services have therefore, and in accordance with the recommendations of the Industrial R&D Advisory Committee of the European Commission (IRDAC) from September 1996, undertaken a major research project on how to set up an organisational network for the regular and continuous collection, monitoring and analyses concerning all services affecting the competitiveness of Industry. In a first phase, the viability of this organisational set-up will be tested by identifying and implementing a survey tool which in the future can be used in a widening and deepening of the present exercise in order to guide policy actions with the aim of improving the competitiveness of European enterprises.

The scope of this project is considerably wider than the traditional definition of Business Services. It encompasses all Industry Value Added Services in the primary value chain (RDT, engineering, logistics, distribution, subcontracting, after-sales etc.) and the support value chain (traditional Business Services, financing, industrial vocational training, communications etc.). Focus is on the demand side for Industry Value Added Services in a first attempt to gain information on how new and emerging services are created by demand and to learn more about the balances and shifts between externalisation/in-house provision of services.

The intention should not be to create yet another institution or agency at Community level. The objective should be to organise a low cost network of existing players in this field and to build on existing structures at Community and national level with the participation of Industry. *Depending on the results of the project, consideration will be given to the possible enlargement of the future Communication on Industrial Competitiveness and Business Services to cover all Industry Value Added Services.*

Chapter 7	**Conclusions**

A. Data and information

The foundations for a better insight into the situation of European Business Services and their contribution to industrial competitiveness have been laid, but important statistical and analytical tasks lie ahead before policy conclusions can be drawn.

In the statistical field national statistical institutes must consolidate the setting up of national business registers and other EU regulatory statistical frameworks. In co-operation with EUROSTAT, new variables and performance indicators must be defined and an appropriate methodology for future work must be sought, building on recent experiences. Further EU resources, although at a relatively modest level, are needed in this field if progress is to be made in a short time-span. Industry itself must cooperate in the collection of user-friendly data in their own interest.

A number of important research projects on Business Services has been initiated and the definition of an overall research strategy is under way. *It is of prime importance to seek a continuous and dynamic development in this field* in order to avoid that research is only conducted as scattered once-off and uncoordinated initiatives. The value of research on Business Services can only be ascertained by following comparative trends and developments on a time-scale.

It is the hope that sufficient progress in the above-mentioned areas will permit the elaboration of a more comprehensive analysis of the situation of Business Services in the planned Commission Communication to the Council in the second half of 1998 during the Austrian presidency. In this connection, *it will be considered whether it is viable to enlarge the scope of the forthcoming Communication to cover all Industry Value Added Services* and not just the traditional Business Services sector.

B. Policy issues

On the basis of the above-mentioned analytical data the future Communication will also attempt to deal with some preliminary policy recommendations.

As indicated in previous chapters of this report a number of issues are seriously hampering manufacturing and service enterprises' access to competitive Business Services. The following policy issues which need detailed treatment in the forthcoming Communication have been identified:

- Organisational and operational issues in the definition of a long-term EU-strategy to ensure a comprehensive and dynamic approach to the situation of the Business Services sector;

- National and Internal Market access barriers as well as restrictions on access to third country markets;

- Other barriers to competition, i.e. price fixing, market control, excess regulation, lack of liberalisation, etc.;

- The role of and the targeting of Community policies on Business Services in particular in the fields of Research and Technological Development, Structural Policy and Training;

- Promotion of quality standards amongst Business services companies;

- Review of public procurement regimes;

- The role and competition from public support services in relation to private services;

- The role of national and Community administrations in providing general and specific data and information, facts about markets and interpretation of national and Community policies to Business Services providers and customers.

Annex 1   Overview of all tradable services

Public utilities(*)	Producer services			Consumer services	
	Business Services(**)	**Financial services**	**Distribution**	**Welfare services**	**Household services**
Transport	Computer and related services	Banking	Retail	Education and training	Restaurants and Hotels
– road		Other credit institutions	Wholesale		
– rail	Professional services		Intermediaries	Health	Repairs
– international waterways	Marketing services	Insurance		Social security	Travel agencies etc.
– postal	Technical services	Real estate			Recreation and other cultural activities
– sea-transport	Renting and leasing services	Pension schemes			
– air-transport		Venture and risk capital etc.			Home services
Telecommunications and ICT services	Labour recruitment and provision of personnel				Personal services
Energy	Operational services				Other services
– electricity	Other Business Services				
– gas					
Water					

(*) The term public *services* has been abandoned in favour of *utilities* to underline that these services, in the present situation of partial liberalisation, are not always *delivered* by public but always *utilised* by the public.

(**) Official statistical definition. Conceptually RDT, industrial training and logistics belong to this group.

Definition of business services by NACE Rev1

Subsector: Computer and related services

72.10   Hardware consultancy

This class includes:
- consultancy on type and configuration of hardware and associated software application:
  - analyzing the users' needs and problems and presenting the best solution

This class excludes:
- *hardware consultancy carried out by computer producing or selling units cf. 30.02, 51.64, 52.48*

72.20   Software consultancy and supply

This class includes:
- analysis, design and programming of systems ready to use:
  - analysis of the user's needs and problems, consultancy on the best solution
  - development, production, supply and documentation of order-make software based on orders from specific users
  - development, production, supply and documentation of ready-made (non-customized) software
  - writing of programs following directives of the user

This class excludes:
- *reproduction of non-customized software cf. 22.33*
- *software consultancy related to hardware consultancy cf. 72.10*

72.30   Data processing

This class includes:
- processing of data employing either the customer's or a proprietary program:
  - complete processing of data
  - data entry services
- management and operation on a continuing basis of data processing facilities belonging to others

72.40   Data base activities

This class includes data base related activities:
- data base development: assembly of data from one or more sources
- data storage: preparation of a computer record for such information in a predetermined format
- data base availability: provision of data in a certain order or sequence, by on-line data retrieval or accessibility (computerized management) to everybody or to limited users, sorted on demand

72.50   Maintenance and repair of office, accounting and computing machinery

72.60   Other computer related activities

Subsector: Professional services

74.11   Legal activities

This class includes:
- legal representation of one party's interest against another party, whether or not before courts or other judicial bodies by, or under supervision of, persons who are members of the bar:
  - advice and representation in civil cases
  - advice and representation in criminal actions
- advice and representation in connection with labour disputes
- general counselling and advising, preparation of legal documents:
  - articles of incorporation, partnership agreements or similar documents in connection with company formation
  - patents and copyrights
  - preparation of deeds, wills, trusts etc.
- activities of notary public, notaries, bailiffs, arbitrators, examiners and referees

This class excludes:
- *arbitration and conciliation between labour and management cf. 74.14*
- *law court activities cf. 75.23*

74.12   Accounting, book-keeping and auditing activities; tax consultancy

This class includes:
- recording of commercial transactions from businesses or others
- preparation of financial accounts, examination of such accounts and certification of their accuracy
- preparation of personal and business income tax returns
- advisory activities and representation (other than legal representation) on behalf of clients before tax authorities

This class excludes:
- *data processing and tabulation activities even for accounting purposes cf. 72.30*
- *management consultancy such as design of accounting systems, cost accounting programmes, budgetary control procedures cf. 74.14*
- *bill collection cf. 74.84*

74.14 Business and management consultancy services

This class includes:
- General management consulting services
- Financial management consulting services (except corporate tax)
- Marketing management consulting services
- Human resources management consulting services
- Production management consulting services
- Public relations services
- Other management consulting services
- Other management-related service
- Project management services other than for construction
- Arbitration and conciliation services
- Other management-related services n.e.c.

Subsector: Marketing services

74.13 Market research and public opinion polling

This class includes:
- investigation into market potential, acceptance, and familiarity of products and buying habits of consumers for the purpose of sales promotion and development of new products including statistical analyses of the results
- investigation into collective opinions of the public about political, economic and social issues and statistical analysis thereof

74.40 Advertising

This class includes:
- creation and realization of advertising campaigns
- creating and placing of outdoor advertising, e.g. billboards, panels, bulletins and frames, window dressing, showroom design, car and bus carding, etc.
- media representation, i.e. sale of time and space for various media soliciting advertising

- aerial advertising
- distribution or delivery of advertising material or samples
- provision of spaces for advertising

This class excludes:
- *printing of advertising material cf. 22.22*
- *market research cf. 74.13*
- *public relations activities cf. 74.14*
- *advertising photography cf. 74.81*
- *production of commercial messages for radio, television and film cf. 92*

Subsector: Technical services

74.20 Architectural and engineering activities and related technical consultancy

This class includes:
- consulting architectural activities:
  - building design and drafting
  - supervision of construction
  - town and city planning and landscape architecture
- machinery and industrial plant design
- engineering, project management and technical activities:
  - projects involving civil engineering, hydraulic engineering, traffic engineering
  - projects elaboration and realization relative to electrical and electronic engineering, mining engineering, chemical engineering, mechanical, industrial and systems engineering, safety engineering
- elaboration of projects using air-conditioning, refrigerating, sanitary and pollution control engineering, acoustical engineering etc.
- geological and prospecting activities:
  - surface measurements and observation designed to yield information on subsurface structure and the location of petroleum, natural gas and mineral deposits and of ground water
- weather forecasting activities
- geodetic surveying activities:
  - land surveying activities

- hydrographic surveying activities
- sub-surface surveying activities
- boundary surveying activities
- cartographic and spatial information activities including aerial photography thereof
- industrial and engineering surveying activities

This class excludes:
- *test drilling and testhole boring cf. 45.12*
- *research and development activities cf. 73*
- *technical testing cf. 74.30*
- *interior decorating cf. 74.84*

74.30 Technical testing and analysis

This class includes:
- measuring related to cleanness of water or air, measuring of radioactivity and the like; analysis of potential pollution such as smoke or waste water
- testing activities in the field of food hygiene
- strength and failure testing
- testing of calculations for building elements
- certification of ships, aircraft, motor vehicles, pressurized containers, nuclear plant etc.
- periodic road safety testing of motor vehicles

Subsector: Renting and leasing services

71.10 Renting of automobiles

This class includes:
- renting and operational leasing of self-drive private cars and light vans up to 3.5 tonnes

This class excludes:
- *financial leasing cf. 65.21*

71.21 Renting of other land transport equipment

This class includes:
- renting and operational leasing of land transport equipment without drivers except automobiles:
  - railroad vehicles

- trucks, haulage tractors, trailers and semi-trailers
- motorcycles, caravans and campers etc..

This class also includes:
- renting of containers

This class excludes:
- *renting or leasing of vehicles or trucks with driver cf. 60.2*
- *financial leasing cf. 65.21*
- *renting of bicycles cf. 71.40*

71.22 Renting of water transport equipment

This class includes:
- renting and operational leasing of water transport equipment such as commercial boats and ships, without operator

This class excludes:
- *renting of water transport equipment with operator cf. 61*
- *financial leasing cf. 65.21*
- *renting of pleasure-boats cf. 71.40*

71.23 Renting of air transport equipment

This class includes:
- renting and operational leasing of air transport equipment without operator

This class excludes:
- *renting of air transport equipment with operator cf. 62*
- *financial leasing cf. 65.21*

71.31 Renting of agricultural machinery and equipment

This class includes:
- renting and operational leasing of agricultural and forestry machinery and equipment without operator:
  - renting of products produced by group 29.3, such as agricultural tractors etc.

This class excludes:
- *renting of this machinery or equipment with operator cf. 01.4*
- *financial leasing cf. 65.21*

71.32 Renting of construction and civil engineering machinery and equipment

This class includes:
- renting and operational leasing of construction and civil engineering machinery and equipment without operator
- renting of scaffolds and work platforms without erection and dismantling

This class excludes:
- *renting of this machinery or equipment with operator cf. 45.50*
- *financial leasing cf. 65.21*

71.33 Renting of office machinery and equipment including computers

This class includes:
- renting and operational leasing of office machinery and equipment including computers, without operator:
  - computing machinery and equipment

Subsector: Labour recruitment and provision of personnel

74.50 Labour recruitment and provision of personnel

This class includes:
- personnel search, selection referral and placement in connection with employment supplied to the potential employer or to the prospective employee:
  - formulation of job descriptions
  - screening and testing of applicants
  - investigation of references etc.
- executive search and placement activities (headhunters)
- labour contracting activities:
  - supply to others, chiefly on a temporary basis, of personnel hired by, and whose emoluments are paid by, the agency

This class excludes:
- *activities of farm labour contractors cf. 01.4*

- *activities of personal theatrical or artistic agents cf. 74.84*
- *motion picture, television and other theatrical casting activities cf. 92.72*

Subsector: Operational services

74.60 Investigation and security activities

This class includes:
- investigation activities
- activities of private investigators
- surveillance, guard and other protective activities :
  - transport of valuables
  - bodyguard activities
  - street patrol, guard and watchman activities for apartment buildings, offices, factories, construction sites, hotels, theatres, dance halls etc.
  - store detective activities
  - monitoring by mechanical or electrical protective devices
- consultancy in the field of industrial, household and public service security
- training of dogs for security reasons

This class excludes:
- *installation of alarm systems cf. 45.31*
- *investigation in connection with insurance cf. 67.20*

74.70 Industrial cleaning

This class includes:
- interior cleaning of buildings of all types, including offices, factories, shops, institutions and other business and professional premises and multi-unit residential buildings
- window cleaning
- chimney cleaning and cleaning of fire-places, stoves, furnaces, incinerators, boilers, ventilation ducts and exhaust units

This class also includes:
- disinfecting and exterminating activities for buildings, ships, trains etc.
- cleaning of trains, buses, planes etc.

This class excludes:
- *agricultural pest control cf. 01.41*

- *steam cleaning, sand blasting and similar activities for building exteriors cf. 45.45*
- *cleaning of new buildings after construction cf. 45.45*
- *carpet and rug shampooing, drapery and curtain cleaning cf. 93.01*
- *activities of domestics cf. 95.00*

Subsector: Other business services

74.81 Photographic activities

This class includes:
- commercial and consumer photograph production:
  - portrait photography for passports, school, weddings etc.
  - photography for commercials, publishers, fashion, real estate or tourism purposes
  - aerial photography
- film processing:
  - developing, printing and enlarging from client-taken negatives or cine films
  - mounting of slides
  - copying and restoring or transparency retouching in connection with photographs

This class also includes:
- operation of photo coin-operated machines

This class excludes:
- *processing motion picture film related to the motion picture and television industries cf. 92.11*

74.82 Packaging activities

This class includes:
- packaging activities, whether or not this involves an automated process:
  - filling of aerosols
  - bottling of liquids, including beverages and food
  - packaging of solids (blister packaging, foil covered etc.)
  - labelling, stamping and imprinting
  - parcel packing and gift wrapping

This class excludes:
- *packing activities incidental to transport cf. 63.40*

74.83 Secretarial and translation activities

This class includes:
- stenographic and mailing activities:
  - typing
  - other secretarial activities such as transcribing from tapes or discs
  - copying, blue printing, multigraphing and similar activities
  - envelope addressing, stuffing, sealing and mailing, mailing list compilation, etc., including for advertising material
- translation and interpretation

This class also includes:
- proof-reading

This class excludes:
- *database activities cf 72.40*
- *bookkeeping activities cf. 74.12*

74.84 Other business activities n.e.c.

This class includes :
- bill collecting, credit rating in connection with an individual's or firm's credit-worthiness or business practices
- business brokerage activities, i.e. arranging for the purchase and sale of small and medium-sized businesses, including professional practices
- appraisal activities other than for real estate and insurance
- fashion design related to textiles, wearing apparel, shoes, jewellery, furniture and other interior decoration and other fashion goods as well as other personal or household goods
- trading stamp activities
- activities of interior decorators
- activities of fair, exhibition and congress organizers
- activities of stand designers

This class also includes:
- activities carried on by agents and agencies on behalf of individuals usually involving the obtaining of engagements in motion picture, theatrical production or other entertainment or sports attractions and the placement of books, plays, artworks, photographs, etc., with publishers, producers, etc

This class excludes:
- *credit card activities cf. 65*
- *machinery and industrial plant design cf. 74.20*
- *display of advertisement and other advertising design cf. 74.40*

Matrix of Dimension for new studies within Business Services

	SECTORAL SCOPE		GEOGRAPHICAL SCOPE			SPECIFIC SCOPE					
	Manufacturing	Services	Regions	Nations	Meta-regions	Globalisation	SMEs	Employment ratio	Technological development	Outsourcing	Obstacles to Trade
IT Services											
Professional services											
Marketing services											
Technical services											
Renting and leasing services											
Labour recruit and provision of pers.											
Operational services											
Other Business Services											

Source: Hanneman Moeller

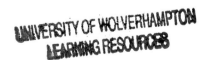

European Commission

The Contribution of Business Services to Industrial Performance
A Common Policy Framework

Luxembourg: Office for Official Publications of the European Communities

1999 — 74 pp. — 21 x 29.7 cm

ISBN 92-828-6670-X